FERDINAND
King of the Two Sicilies

MEMOIRS

OF THE

SECRET SOCIETIES
OF THE SOUTH OF ITALY,

PARTICULARLY THE

CARBONARI

by

Jakob Salomon Bartholdy

(ATTRIBUTED)

TRANSLATED FROM THE ORIGINAL MS.

London
Spradabach Publishing
2023

Spradabach Publishing
BM Box Spradabach
London WC1N 3XX

*Memoirs of the Secret Societies of the South of Italy,
and Particularly the Carbonari*

First Spradabach edition published 2023
© Spradabach Publishing 2023

Interior design by Alex Kurtagic

ISBN 978-1-909606-43-2

British Library Cataloguing-in-Publication Data:
A catalogue record for this book is available from the British Library.

Table of Contents

Note on This Edition

The present is volume is based on the 1821 edition printed in London by John Murray. It is reproduced in its entirety.

The spelling and punctuation are as in the original, but the Italian words and phrases, some of which appeared in Roman type, have been more consistently italicised. Proper names that appeared uncapitalised have been capitalised, and the capitalisation criteria has been homogenised following modern convention. Extensive quotes have been set in block quotes.

A number of editorial footnotes have been added, and marked out accordingly to distinguish them from the translators'. Editorial footnotes, however, have been kept to a minimum.

All but one of the illustrations included in the original, which appeared in the form of fold-outs, have been included, albeit with some imperfections due to the age of the original medium. One of the illustrations, which had to be omitted due to there not being an usable image available at the time of going to print, will be included in a future edition.

A comprehensive index, absent in the original, has been generated.

Preface

t is neither without hesitation, nor a full conviction of the inconveniences that may possibly await him, that the Author of these *Memoirs on the Secret Societies of the South of Italy* has resolved on making them public.

If those who undertake to write the less thorny episodes of contemporary history be exposed to virulent attacks from the vanity or the susceptibility of those individuals of whom they cannot avoid speaking without praise, what may not be looked for when whole sects form the subject;— sects, which some consider as the focus of crimes and atrocity, while others look upon them as the asylums of virtue, and the place of refuge for oppressed patriotism!

But the hope of being useful to humanity ought to overcome any repugnance founded on personal considerations. It is the mystery which envelopes these Societies—it is the notions of extraordinary importance attached to them, which prevent impartiality, and may mislead those who are called upon to be judges in the cause, and to deliberate on the means for neutralizing the evil in the first instance, and for repressing it in future.

The veil of secrecy being removed from these Societies, it will readily be perceived, that the prison and the scaffold are not the arms with which to oppose them: and that persecution can only tend to exasperate the multitude to a degree which may lead them to sacrifice their repose, their conscience, and their duty to the state, in order to maintain institutions puerile in themselves, yet dangerous because they open a vast field of influence, to the enthusiast, to the impostor, and to the ambitious man.

The history of the Carbonari of Naples forms the principal subject of the present work. Their existence has been known for many years; but it was the revolution of July, 1820, which brought them into full daylight.

Victorious and exclusive during the first months of that revolution, they imagined that they had no cause for further concealment. They boasted of their success; they revealed their secret proceedings; they promulgated decrees, and posted up proclamations. The press multiplied their Catechisms, the Transactions of their Societies, and the results of their deliberations. Their Patents and their Symbols were sold publicly.

From these sources, the Author, who never belonged to any secret society, not even to Freemasonry, which is tolerated and protected throughout the greater part of Europe, has drawn the materials of his work. They encreased upon him as he arranged them; but as they did not present themselves either chronologically, or in the order of their respective importance, he was obliged perpetually to correct, abridge, and transpose, which has occasioned a confusion of compilation, a want of unity in the cast, which could only have been corrected by means of leisure and careful revision. The Author has preferred sacrificing these advantages, to that of seizing the favourable moment for publication.

He must further observe, that the original is French, although it is not his mother tongue. He made use of it on account of his English translator thereby renouncing all pretension to elegance of style. It was of too much consequence to him to bring out his work first in London. The continent is accustomed to receive the truth with less distrust when it proceeds from Great Britain. It is a homage we owe to her: let her permit us to wish that we may soon participate with her in this honourable privilege.

The Author, living at a distance from the translator, has not had the advantage of comparing the work with the original manuscript, or of giving him those verbal explanations which might often have been essentially necessary. This is an additional reason for not refusing him the indulgence he lays claim to.

After all, it will be perceived, that he relies wholly on the interest of the subject, and on the consciousness of never having altered facts, to adapt them either to prejudice or to theory.

He will give his name when the original is published.

Naples, 26th January.

Translator's Preface

If the Author solicits indulgence on account of the desultory mode in which he collected his materials, the Translator can claim no less. The original manuscript was transmitted to him in detached portions; he was frequently left to find out the probable place of the several paragraphs and documents to be inserted in various parts of the work, without a possibility of consulting the Author. Besides this disadvantage, and that occasioned by the circumstance that the Author himself did not write in his native language, there is another with regard to various passages translated from the Italian, such as, the Declarations, Laws,

&c. of the Carbonari. The originals of these are mostly written in a peculiar dialect, often by very illiterate persons, and almost always printed very carelessly, so that in many instances the sense can only be conjectured.

The Translator has ventured to add a few notes, which are marked *T*.

List of the Books and Pamphelts Referred to in the Memoirs of the Carbonari

1. *Catechismo di un B. C. in Grade di Appren-dente.* Napoli, 1820. Dai torchj di un B. C. e M. (30 pagine.) (In fine si legge: Collazionato e trovato regolare; Il B. C. O. (Oratore) presso la R. V. i figlj di Erennio, All'O. di B. Sign. Cassito Romoaldo.
2. *Catechismo di un B. C. in Grado di Appren-dente.*—12 pagine, senza indicazione di data e stampatore.
3. *Apertura dei Sacri Travaglj, per use del B. C. N. N. figlio della R. V. sotto il T. .D.* (titolo dis-tintivo) .... contiene: ᵃ) Apertura dei Travaglj di 1º Grado, p. l6; ᵇ) Spiega del Quadro Simbol-ico, p. 8; ᶜ) Catechismo, p. 13; ᵈ) Apertura de'

Travaglj di 2do Grado, p. 16; ^{e}) Costituzione dell' Ordine della B. C. in Napoli, p. 32.

4. *Apertura dei Travaglj di 2do Grado*, p. 15. senza indicaz. di luogo e stampat.

5. Istruzioni sul 1° Gr. di Appr. Carb. redatto dal Gr. M. della R. V. all' O. di Napoli. Pasquale Tavassi; sotto il titolo distintivo: *I Liberi Pitagorici.* Napoli, 1820. Dai Torchj di Gius. Severino, p. 24.

6. Istruzioni del 2do Gr. di M. Carb.; dall'istesso Autore ed Editore delle precedente Istruzioni.

7. *Travaglj del 3ro Grado*, p. 8. (senza indicaz. di luogo e stampat.)

8. *Codice di Carboneria*, Parte I^{a} al 1° Gr. degli Apprendenti.

9. *Il Mentore dei Carbonari.*

10. Diplomi stampati ed incisi, dei BB. CC. di 1° e 2do Grado.

11. *Nuovo Statuto Organico della Carboneria della R.* (Repubblica) *Lucana Occidentale, (Principato citra), sanzionato nella gran Dieta dell' anno II.* (1818)—O. Centrale di Salerno. Dalla Tipografia dell. R. L. Oc. p. 12. qu^{to}.

12. *Tavola della Gran Dieta C. straordinaria dell'anno III. della R. Lucana Occidentale.* Tipograf. della R. L. Oc. p. 30. qu^{to}.

13. *Giornale della R. Lucana Occidentale*, N°. I. e II. Tipogr. della R. L. Oc.

14. *Organizzazione del Potere Giudiziario, sanzionata dai Rappresentanti del Popolo Carbonaro, della Luc. Occid.* p. 14.

15. *Codice di Rito Giudiziario*, sanzionato come sopra; P-8.

17.[1] *Costituzione del Popolo Carbonaro della Repubblica Lucana Orientale.* Anno I. stampat. a Cosenza; Libertà, Eguaglianza.

18. *Breve e fidele Esposizione de' primi Fatti avvenuti nella Luc. Orientale dal giorno 4 al 7mo Luglio, per lo Stabilimento della Costituzione.*

19. *Giornale Patriotico della Luc. Orientale:* Potenza, dai 10, 20, e 30 Luglio e 10 Agosto.

20. *Risposta ad una Diatriba del di 11mo Agosto, &c. &c. dal Inte. G^{le} Fr. Pignatelli Strongoli.*

21. *Cenno dei Fatti accaduti nel Regno di Napoli, nei primi giorni di Luglio del 1820 del Inte G^{lo} Fr. Pignatelli Strongoli.*

22. *Cenno Istorico su i Fatti che hanno preceduto e prodotto il Movimento del Battaglione Sacro di Nola.*

23. *Rimostranza della Societa de' Carbonari al Sommo Pontefice Pio VII.* Napoli, 20 Sett. 1820. pr. mandato, G.A.

24. *La Minerva Napolitana, 1mo Quaderno . . . la Nobiltà ed i Carbonari.*

25. *L'Amico della Costituzione*, fascicolo I. 26. Processo Romano contro i Congiurati di Macerata de 1817: Ristretto presentato dal Relatore (Leggieri) alia Congregazione Criminale. Roma, 1818: Stamperia della Camera Apostolica.

27. *Memoires sur le Royaume de Naples, &c.* par le Comte Or. d'Orloff. Paris. 1819.

---

1   Item 16 is missing in the original. —Ed.

28. *Histoire des Sociétés Secrètes de l'Armée Françoise*: Paris, 1815.
29. Joh. V. Müller. Aug. *Wellgeschichte.*
30. Baillet, *Vie des Saints*; Vie de St. Theobald: Paris, 1704.
31. *La Vita di S. Teobaldo, Presbitero, Eremita, e Confessore: trad, dal Latino dal B. C. Giacinto di Mattia.* Napoli, Agosto, 1820.
32. *Poesie diverse Carboniche*, &c.; Poesie di una Cugina Giardiniera.
33, *Notizie sulla Condotta politica di Gius. Zurlo*; terza Edizione correttissima. Napoli, 1820.
34. Marangoni, *Oggetti Profani adattati ai Sacri*, &c. &c.
35. Editto del Card. Pacca, Pro-Segretario di Stato di S. S. del 15ᵐᵒ Agosto, 1814, contr. le Società Segrete.
36. Rapporto del Ministro della Polizia Gˡᵉ (Saliceti) sulla Congiura ordita nel 1807, contr. L'Armata Francese, nel Regno di Napoli, e contr. la persona e gli stati di S. M. Gius. Napoleone.
37. L'istesso Rapporto, ristampato, ed accompagnato di Note dal Principe di Canosa.
38. Capitolazione tra la Truppa de' Carabinieri Ponteficj, e i'Armata Carbonica Costituzionale di Benevento: nella Stamperia nazionale di Benevento; (un foglio).
39. *Indirizzo al P. N.* (Parlamento Nazionale); presso Pasquale Tizzano, Str. Cisterna dell' Olio Nº. 26: (emanato dall'Alta Vendita di Napoli.)

40. *Al Parlamento Nazionale delle due Sicilie*; (Indirizzo degli Uffiziali Napolitani, destituiti come Codardi nel 1815, in seguito di una Sentenza della Commissione Militare preseduta prima dal Amato G^{le} ed indi dal G^{le} Gugl. Pepe.) Presso lo stampatore Gabr. di Filippis, Salita Stella N°. 10.

41. La R. Assemblea Generale dei Carbonari, a tutti li BB. CC. della Due Sicilie S. S. S. O . . . di Napoli, 24 Ott. 1820. (Questo é Proclama, per eccitare i Carbonari ad impedire i molti Furti, che da qualche tempo si commettono sulle pubbliche Strade.)

42. *Breve Idea della Carboneria, sua Origine nel Regno di Napoli, suo Scopo, sua Persecuzione, e Causa che fe' nascere la Setta de' Calderari;* Del Dottor in Legge Pasquale Tonelli. Napoli, 1820, pr. P. Tizzano. 8 pagine.

43. *Il Carbonaro Istruito*, Traduzione dal Francese: Mila no, 1815. pp. 63: (Milano parve luogo supposto.)

Precede la Vita di S. Teobaldo, poi i Travagli del 1° Grado che non si distinguono in niente, di cio eh' ensegua il Catechismo deila Carboneria, &c. II Giuramento e assolutamente Tistesso.

All'occasione del 2do, Brindisi a Francesco I. (p. 47.) si legge in nota sotto la pagine. "Questo Re fu il padre delle lettere, il prottettore della Carboneria, in guisa che fece in essa iniziare tutt' i suoi maresciali, da lui sempre chiamati coll' onorevole titolo de cugini.

Seguetano dopo il Catechismo e le Spiegazioni della Obligazioni particolari, varie canzoni intitolati: la Forna e la Fede; 2) la Speranza; 3) la Carita; 4) la Rivizione; 5) la Morte.

44. *Il Carbonaro Istruito*, Traduzione dal Francese. Milano, 1815, pp. 63.

45. *I Piffari di Montagna, ossio Cenno estemporaneo sulla Congiura del Principe di Canosa, e sopra i Carbonari.* Dublino, nel Maggio del 1820.

46. *Memorie del Avvocato Carlo Quarto nella Causa dei tre arrestati, Guglielmo Paladini, Salv. Vecchiarelli e Pasquale Maenza,* &c. &c.

47. Circolare dal Ministro degli Affari Ecclesiastici D. G. Troyse, Agli Arcivescovi e Vescovi, &c. (vid. il Censore, Nº. 18: il23 Genajo, 1821.)

Memoirs of the Carbonari

It is probable that the Society of the Carbonari, as it actually exists in the Kingdom of Naples, is of comparatively recent formation, and that it has originated since the French revolution. But as individuals are apt to claim a descent from illustrious ancestors, so associations love to consider themselves of remote antiquity, and are all desirous of proving their connection with the order of the Templars, or with the famous subjects of the Old Man of the Mountain.

The traditions of the Carbonari yield to none in this respect, and it is from the history of Germany that they derive the proofs of their antiquity. The necessity of mutual assistance, it is said, induced the colliers,[1] who inhabited the vast forests of Germany, to unite themselves against robbers and enemies. By conventional signs known only to themselves, they claimed and afforded mutual assistance. The criminal enterprize of Conrad de Kauffungen, to carry off the Saxon princes, failed through the intervention of the colliers. And at a period much more recent, a Duke of Wurtemburg was compelled by them, under threat of death, to abolish certain forest laws, considered as oppressive or cruel.[2]

These associations, in the course of time, acquired more consistency, and spread themselves over Germany, France, and the Netherlands. Their secret, and the oath which bound them together, was called the faith of the colliers. Important services rendered to the members of the order, sometimes, though rarely, procured, to persons of rank, admissions into its body; and it is asserted that several members of the parliaments of France were enrolled in it in the years 1770-1790.

The society of Hewers (*Fendeurs*) resembled that of the Colliers. Among their symbols of initia-

---

1   Literally Charcoal-burners, or Charrers.
2   The forest laws have given rise to frequent and violent commotions in Germany, as well as in England. The insurrection of the German peasantry, headed by the reformer Muricer, 1524, pretended to have the double object of reformation in religion, and the abrogation of the oppressive forest laws.

tion, we find the trunk of an old tree, together with other allusions to their occupations in the woods.[3] A book which excited some attention in France, namely, *The History of the Secret Societies,which had in view the Destruction of the Government of Buonaparte*—Paris, 1815,[4] contains a curious note on the origin of the Carbonari. It is, at once, an apology for the institution, and for its object; concerning which the author seems to be thoroughly informed. Of the whole work it is the passage where the details are most interesting. He asserts that the association of Charbonniers, or Bucherons, has long existed in the French department of the Jura, and among the inhabitants of the neighbouring mountains; and that it is there called Cousinship, or Good Cousinship, (*Le Bon Cousinage*). It was revived and put in activity under the reign of Bonaparte, nominally by the Marquis de Champagne.

At the feasts of the Carbonari, the Grand Master drinks to the health of Francis I. King of France, the founder of the order.[5] An historical essay in

---

3   For an account of the occupation of the Charrers, or Colliers, see the story of Martin Waldeck, in the popular novel of the Antiquary.

4   Charles Nodier, *Histoire des sociétés secrètes de l'Arme, et des conspirations militaires qui ont eu pour objet la destruction du goverment de Bonaparte* (Paris: Gide Fils, 1815); of which there is an English version, *History of the Secret Societies of the Army, and of the Military Conspiracies, which had for their object the destruction of the Government of Bonaparte* (London: Longman, Hurst, Rees, Orme and Brown, 1815) —Ed.

5   2 Brind. Il G. M. lo porta a Francesco 1mo Re di Francia, (Fon-

the "Code of Carbonarism" contains an amusing account of the origin of the order, and of the initiation of its royal protector; and characteristically concludes, by referring the reader to the Abbe Barruel's *History of Jacobinism*.[6] It may be taken as a fair specimen of the many compositions of the sort with which the Neapolitan Carbonari have gratified the public.

HISTORICAL ESSAY ON THE ORIGIN OF CARBONARISM[7]

---

datore dell' Ordine). *See*, Il Mentore di un B. C. C. App. (Buon Cugino Carbonaro Apprendente), p. 51.

6   Augustin Barruel, *Memoirs Illustrating the History of Jacobinism*, 4 vols. (London: Hudson and Goodwin, 1798-9). —Ed.

7   The following is a faithful copy: the orthography of the original is preserved. The sense is occasionally guessed at in the translation.

Saggio Istorico sull'Origine delta Carboneria

L'Istoria della turbolenza nella Scozia, allorchè la Regina Isabella[a] fisso un epoca della Carboneria, molti illustri uomini sottratti del gioco (giogo) della tirannia, si ricoverarono nelle foreste. Per allontanare ogni sospetto di criminose adunanze, si posero a tagliare le legna, ed a fare de' Carboni, *unico prodotto commerciale in Iscozia*—Con questo favore essi si riconducevano ne' paesi, ed esponendo i Carboni a Vendita, portando l'etimologia delle loro unioni a' V. C. (veri Carbonari). In tal guisa ottenero l'agio di rincontrarsi con i loro partegiani, e communicarsi vicendevolmente *i sentimenti de' loro piani*. Si riconoscevano pero con segni, tatto, e parole; non essendo poi delle abitazioni costruirono delle baracche di legna con figura quadrilunga. Stabilirono un governo che emano dei regolamenti—Questo governo rappresentato da tre persone era triennale, tenente una Vendita di legislazione, una di amminrini-

istrazione, e la terza giudiziaria, che si chiama Alta Vendita.[b]
Si divisero in tante baracche ciascuna veniva eretta da un buon Cugino che non era, se non che il primo tra gli eguali, che communicava coll' Alta Vendita e che chiamavasi G. M. (gran maestro).

Si rivenne nelle foreste un eremita di nome Teobaldo; cestui si unisce con essi e ne favorisce l'intrapresa. *Si rende aimnirabile*, ed e proclamato protettore dei B. C. C. Così pacifici questi uomini filantropi *menevano* i loro giorni e si univano in alcuni stabiliti tempi.

Avenne che Francesco 1mo, Re di Francia, andando a caccia ne' confini del regno della parte di Scozia, inseguendo una fiera si allontauo dai suoi corteggiani; si fè notte e si disperse per la foresta. S'imbatte in una di queste baracche, chiese ricovero e gli fu accordato, somministrandogli unanimamente tutto il bisognevole. Ammirò Francesco I. il contento di questi uomini C. C. e la loro mistica disciplina. Crede di trovare cosa di misterioso e di singolare, e si manifesta Re di Francia. Domandò con istanza di conoscere i loro misterj e qual *fusse* lo scopo delle loro unioni. Viene soddisfatto e ne rimase *ammirato*. Chiede di voler esser iniziato e promesse *divenirne* il loro protettore. Si gli accorda un tal favore (!) L'indomani fu restituito in seno de' cacciatori che desolati lo andavano cercando avendolo smarrito. Tornato in Francia adempì esattamente il giuramento. Si dichiara protettore de' C. C. e ne moltiplica il numero, che in seguito si distese in Germania ed indi in Inghilterra.

Chiunque de' B. C. C. desidera di avere un numero maggiore de notizie rapporto al nutrimento;, al progresso ed all' espansione della setta C. (*Carbonica*) potra leggere: *L'Histoire du Jacohinisme* di Barruel, che con somma accuratezza e diligenza e stata tradotta e stampata in Italia, ed in prosieguo e stata anche diligentemente tradotta, annotata, e stampata in Napoli.[c]

a   There was no Isabella, Queen of Scotland, contemporary with Francis I. of France. The Isabel, whose adventures, while living in the woods with banished men, the nobles of the country, might be a subject for romance, was the first wife of Robert Bruce, and must have died within the first twelve years of the fourteenth century. It is, however, scarcely worth while to search for Queen Isabella, since the Scotland she reigned over is certainly not part of Britain, if Francis reached its woods, while hunting, or if its

5

During the troubles in Scotland, in Queen Isabella's time, which formed an æra in Carbonarism, many illustrious persons having escaped from the yoke of tyranny took refuge in the woods. In order to avoid all suspicion of criminal association, they employed themselves in cutting wood and making charcoal (the only commercial produce of Scotland). Under pretence of carrying their charcoal for sale, they introduced themselves into the villages, and bearing the name of real Carbonari (*Colliers*), they easily met their partisans, and mutually communicated their different plans. They recognized each other by signs, by touch, and by words; and as there were no habitations in the forest, they constructed huts of an oblong form, with branches of trees. They established a government, which issued laws. This government consisted of three persons: their office was triennial, and they presided over three vendite, or lodges; one legislative, another administrative, and the third judicial. This last was called the Alta Vendita.

These vendite were subdivided into a number of *Baracche*, each erected by a Good Cousin of some distinction among his companions, who communicated with the Alta Vendita, and was styled the Grand Master.

---

principal produce is the charcoal of its forests. —T.

b   Vendita may be translated Lodge—it is literally place cf sale, or market; Baracca in Italian and Spanish is a hut, or tent: hence the word barrack, a temporary dwelling. —T.

c   Codice di Caiboueria, Parte Ima. ul Imo grado dcgli A. (Apprendenti) Londia (Napoli).

There dwelt in the forest a hermit of the name of Theobald: he joined them, and favoured their enterprize. He captivated their admiration, and was proclaimed protector of the Carbonari. Thus peaceably, these philanthropists passed their days, and met at certain appointed times.

It happened that Francis I. King of France, hunting on the *frontiers of his kingdom, next to Scotland,* in following a wild beast, parted from his courtiers. Night came on, and he lost himself in the forest. He stumbled upon one of the baracche and asked for shelter; it was granted, and the Good Cousins unanimously ministered to him all that he was in need of. Francis I. admired the happiness of these Carbonari, and their mystic discipline. He thought he saw something mysterious and singular in it, and discovered himself to them as King of France. He earnestly requested to be made acquainted with their secret, and with the object of their association. They gratified him, and he was struck with admiration; and expressed a wish to be initiated into their order, promising to be their protector. The favour was granted, and next morning he was restored to the hunters, who, having missed him, were seeking him in great anxiety. On his return to France, he scrupulously fulfilled his oath. He declared himself the protector of the Carbonari, and increased their number. The society afterwards spread itself successively over Germany and England. Any G. C. who wishes to have further information respecting the origin, progress, and extension of the sect, may read the *History of Jacobinism* by Barruel, which has been most accurately and carefully translated, and published in Italy; and since diligently re-translated and published with notes at Naples.[8]

* * *

The French branch of the Order derives considerable importance from the adoption of its patron saint in Italy, where he had formerly been little known or honoured. St Theobald has been elected protector of the Society at Naples, as he is of the *Charbonniers* of France.[9] It is he who is invoked by the Good Cousins in their hymns, and who is mystically alluded to in two pieces of verse dedicated

---

8   It will be seen in the course of the work that the religious sectaries which preceded the Reformation were probably the founders of most of the secret societies of Italy, France, and Germany. It is possible, therefore, that the origin of this story is to be found in the protection granted by Louis XII. to the Waldenses, who had taken refuge in Dauphiné. Francis the First suffered their persecution with great reluctance, and on his death-bed enjoined his successor to punish their oppressors. The injunction was disregarded; but though a horrid massacre took place, the mountains of Dauphiné continued to shelter a remnant of the unhappy Waldenses, which occasioned petty disturbances even in the reign of Louis XIV. See Lacretelle, *Guerres de la Religion, also* Mad. de Sevigné's *Letters.* —T.

9   See, at the end of this Memoir, the Life of St. Theobald, extracted from Baillet. *La Vita di S. Teobaldo, tradotta dal Latino d. buon Cugino Giacinto de Mattia*, was published at Naples, August, 1820.

to the Friends (*Agli Amici*) and printed at Naples a few days after the last revolution. The first of these pieces compares the concord of the Carbonari to a sacerdotal and precious ointment.[10]

> *Di unguento tal sacrandosi*
> *Teobaldo al tempio, air ara,*
> *Gli astanti ritrovavansi*
> *Di soavità si cara,*
> *Cosi nostra concordia*
> *E grata al mio Signor.*

The second intimates that "the Friends" participate in the delights of the union, as this ointment spreads itself over the person of St. Theobald.

> *Cosi qualor consagrasi*
> *Per tutto si diffonde*
> *L'unguento odorosissimo*
> *Che Teobaldo infonde,*
> *Pria sulle chiome spargesi*
> *Poi sulla barba lunga,*
> *Finche scorrendo all ultimo*
> *Lembo del manto giunga.*

It appears certain, however, that neither the *Fendeurs* nor the *Charbonniers* ever rose to any importance, or acted any conspicuous part among the secret societies of Europe, till the period of the Revolution. Doubtless such societies

---

10   No translation of these little pieces has been subjoined, as they are both paraphrastic versions of the 1st and 2nd verses of the 133rd psalm.

were in being in Italy, as well as in other countries, before that time; but on the breaking out of that fearful event, they were superseded by others more generally known, and of more importance.

The Free-masons were established in Italy among all ranks. The Illuminati of Weishaupt reckoned among their initiated some of the Knights of Malta, with the celebrated Dolomieu at their head. But the reorganizers of the Carbonari of the present day chose that order in preference, because it suited their plan to gain proselytes chiefly among the middle and lower classes of the people. They acted upon the principle that dictated the clear statement contained in the letter of the Duke of Otranto to the Duke of Wellington, dated January 1, 1816: and which is as follows:—

> The tranquillity of kingdoms does not depend upon the manner in which persons of rank think and act, nor upon the spirit that governs them. Their ambition has no influence if it be not united to some popular interest. Their intrigues and their conspiracies are impotent in their consequences, if not supported by the active interference of the multitude. If the monarch has the attachment and the force of the people on his side, he has nothing to fear from opposition in pubic debates, nor from secret faction. Public quiet depends on the moral direction of the labouring classes who compose the body of the people, and constitute the base of the social edifice. It is these, therefore, that

should be the principal objects of the care and
vigilance of a good police, &c.[11]

The reform, or rather the restoration of the order of Carbonari, is ascribed by the grand masters
at Naples to an unknown officer who had spent
some time in Spain. The next efficient supporter
of the sect, was Maghella, a native of Genoa, of
whom we will give some biographical traits, which
may serve to throw light on his motives for coun-
tenancing and assisting in the renewal of the order
of Carbonari. He was originally employed in the
counting-house of a man of rank and influence in
his native country, whose lady introduced and recommended him to the French authorities.

As minister of police in the Ligurian Republic,
he displayed firmness and talent in some popular
tumults. Murat became acquainted with him during the French campaign in Piedmont, and gave
him his protection and countenance. He was not
equally happy in making an impression on Bonaparte, who, on the annexation of Genoa to France,
only bestowed on him the office of Director of
the Sale of Tobacco. When Murat succeeded Joseph Bonaparte on the throne of Naples, Saliceti,
then minister of police in that kingdom, sent for
Maghella, and employed him in his department
without any ostensible situation. On the sudden

---

11   We find a similar opinion in Cicero's recently discovered trea-
     tise, *De Republica*. T,

death of Saliceti, Maghella obtained his place, with the title of director-general of police, and a seat in the council of state.

Before Bonaparte's Russian campaign in 1812, Maghella had advised Murat to take no part in it; and when the latter returned to Naples in December the same year, much dissatisfied with that disastrous expedition, the same minister did not hesitate to hazard, at a meeting of council held on the occasion, a still more daring opinion. He advised Murat to declare openly against Bonaparte, and to proclaim the independence of Italy; and he dwelt on the favourable chances of such a project under the circumstances of the moment.

The French armies were annihilated, and the allies, but newly and feebly united, in 1813, would have lent their aid most willingly to any new enemy of France. Even at the congress of Prague, seven or eight months later, they did not oppose the independence of Italy, which they then considered as a fresh advantage gained over Napoleon. Some English agents of distinction anxiously diffused this idea in the country, and even acted upon it.

The small French garrisons in the departments of Rome, the lake of Thrasymene, Tuscany, and Genoa would have been easily driven out, and Maghella himself offered to excite a movement in the kingdom of Italy, to put down the government of the Viceroy. The Revolution at Milan on the 20th of April, 1814, has since proved that he did not miscalculate, and that the viceregal government of Eugene Beauharnois was not very firmly established.

That national independence was the object proposed by the Neapolitan propagators of liberty, appears from the deposition of the Count Gallo d'Arpino, who was implicated in the conspiracy of Macerata, 1817. On his examination at the Castle of St. Angelo, he asserted that their maxims were favourable to the papal government, " inasmuch as he (Gallo) remembered to have heard from Zurlo, minister of the interior, and from Salfi, professor of history at Naples, with both of whom he conversed at Pesaro, in April, 1815, during the campaign of Murat against the Austrians,—that it was only necessary to drive out the foreigners, without altering the governments of the country, and that they therefore disapproved of his Holiness absenting himself from his states."[12]

To throw off the yoke of the transalpines, "*cacciare i barbari dall' Italia,*" had been the exhortation directed by Petrarca and Macchiavelli, and by others before and after them, against all foreign powers. It was now pointed exclusively against France. The sovereigns of other countries no longer considered such maxims dangerous. They ventured to repeat them in their proclamations against Bonaparte, from 1809 to 1814. But the cry of Italian independence soon found a more dangerous application, for it is become the rallying

12   Printed minutes of the trial. See Appendix.

word of all factions against the legitimate governments of the country.

Murat was too timid and too irresolute to follow the course pointed out to him by his minister of police: and the French party at Naples sent information of Maghella's sentiments and advice to Paris. Genoa being then considered as part of France, he was claimed as a Genoese, and consequently a French subject, and was accordingly sent to Paris as a prisoner. Napoleon endeavoured in vain to win him over to his interest, and he remained under the surveillance of the police until December, 1813, when the armies of the allies entered upon the French territory. His escape was effected in a daring and romantic manner; and his arrival at Naples contributed much towards determining Murat to declare against his brother-in-law.

Being once more at liberty, he eagerly endeavoured to rouse Italy to independence in 1815; and in the name of Murat he organized the Papal provinces, of which he had taken possession, and it was there that the lodges of the Carbonari were then established, and thence they increased rapidly in the country.

Maghella ought to have been aware, that his schemes for the independence of Italy were most chimerical and impracticable. This consideration, however, was overlooked in his eagerness for the cause; but he must have known Murat too well, to believe, that he was the person who could put such a project in execution. He probably intended to use him as an instrument, whom he could afterwards reject at pleasure. He began by endeavouring to limit the regal power at Naples by a constitution, in order to hold out such an additional bait to the other Italian States, as might induce them to join in his views. The nobility and higher classes of the capital lent themselves readily to his proposals, and the names of the first families are among the signatures to the address printed March, 1815, soliciting a constitution from Joachim, which he had often promised, though without any apparent intention of keeping that promise. The nobles were influenced by motives which are easily explained. They had seen their ancient privileges and their feudal revenues successively disappear; the greater number had been stript of these with very little ceremony, and without indemnification; and as a body, they could offer no resistance to the government. They therefore hoped to find a resource, and their hopes were not unfounded, in a constitutional assembly which it would become their business to manage. Their object was rather to check the royal authority as opposed to the aristocratic interest, than to defend the rights of the people!

The army made common cause with them from motives equally selfish. They were jealous of a great number of French officers of all ranks, employed and often preferred by Murat. They had attempted to procure the removal of these foreigners at various times in vain, and they therefore regarded a national parliament as a remedy for the particular evil of which they had to complain, and hoped that the dismissal of the intruders would be among its first decrees.

The provinces of the kingdom, particularly the Abruzzi and the Calabrias, displayed a feeling of indifference, and even dislike to the great work of the Constitution. They still retained an attachment to King Ferdinand, and an aversion from innovations, the utility of which they could not comprehend. It was to get rid of these sentiments and to gain the people by degrees to the constitutional object without letting them perceive it themselves, that Maghella and his associates resolved to introduce the sect of the Carbonari. This was accomplished; but it became necessary also to deceive Murat and the opposite party. They were assured, therefore, that such an institution would operate powerfully in drawing off the attention of the populace, always prone to rebellion from the remembrance of their ancient sovereigns, and would assist in gaining them over to the new order of things. Meanwhile, the doctrine preached to the inhabitants of the Calabrias and the Abruzzi was as perfectly adapted to their conception as to their inclinations. It depended for effect on the two-fold excitement of religious fanaticism and pecuniary interest; for, while the imitation of Jesus Christ, himself the Grand Master of the Order, was the devotional object proposed, they were shown, at the bottom of the scene, a political change which must infallibly diminish the taxes.

But the Austrian successes under General Bianchi, in 1815, put an end to the political intrigues of Maghella; for he was taken prisoner and sent to a Hungarian fortress. After some time, he was given up to his sovereign, the King of Sardinia, who confined him for twelve months at Fenestrella, and afterwards set him at liberty.

Some persons at Naples imagine that the Tugen-bund (Union of Justice) in Prussia had suggested to Maghella the idea of forming secret societies as a means of directing public opinion against the French; but according to the Minerva Napolitana[13] he might have found examples of such in his own country, with this difference, that they had taken an opposite direction. "The machinations," says that paper,

> of a few cautious, though ambitious persons found means, soon after the year 1790, to spread certain liberal political doctrines among the numerous class of the real Carbonari of Genoa, in order to deliver that flourishing city from the dominion of its oligarchy and to annex it to France. These same doctrines were preached about ten years afterwards among the lower classes of the kingdom of Naples, and the proselytes of that part of Italy, adopting the same denomination (*Carbonari*), which was properly applied to the Genoese colliers, used it in a metaphorical sense to signify a man of small property, or a mere husbandman or artisan!

To give stability to the sect thus introduced at Naples, and to graft it, if we may so speak, on an old stock, in order to force its growth, all Free-ma-

---

13   No. 7

sons were admitted simply by ballot, and out undergoing the preparatory trials required from ordinary candidates!

Hence it is, perhaps, that from the minutes of the proceedings at Rome against the conspirators of Macerata,[14] it appears that all the secret societies of Italy were considered as derived from freemasonry. The members of the court observe, "We had become fully acquainted with the masonic sect during past calamities, which owe their origin to it. The other, that of the Carbonari, was called in just as these calamities were about to cease, as if to increase and perpetuate them. It had its origin and principal seat at Naples, whence it spread to some provinces of the Papal State, and its inauspicious influence had been particularly felt in the Marches. While, in the midst of general peace, this Society was making progress in several cities of Dalmatia, other secret associations no less audaciously erected themselves. The Guelphs extended themselves into Lombardy from the northern provinces of the states of the Church. The Republican brother protectors of French and Lombard origin insinuated themselves into some parts of the Marches. The Adelphi lurk in great secrecy throughout Piedmont; and lastly the Society of the Black Pin (La Spillanera) has attempted to introduce itself into Italy from France. These different denominations, which succeeded each other, were artfully invented not only for the purpose of increasing their se-

14   See App. No. II.

crecy, but to enable their chiefs whenever it suited their purposes, to get rid of members who had been admitted, although of the basest condition, or of such as change of times or circumstances had rendered obnoxious to suspicion. They also served to inform all the initiated at once, of whatever was going on in the way of innovation or reform, to discover their inclinations and opinions, and to keep them in constant activity, that they might be ready and ardent to support, on the first opportunity, a political change agreeable to their wishes.

> In fact, the adherence of any individual to one of the secret societies suffices to ensure his reception with a corresponding rank into all those that may be formed afterwards, so that one sect is always merging in another, while procuring new proselytes. That they are all, however, no other than so many ramifications of Masonry, some of the best informed sectaries themselves allow, and none of them differ essentially as to the object they have in view: viz. —Independence, or, at least, a constitutional government, particularly in Italy.

One consequence of this amalgamation has been the toleration of all the Christian sects which Masonry contained. This is clearly expressed in the fundamental Statute of Carbonarism, in the Western Lucanian Republic,[15] central district of Salerno,

---

15   Principato Citra.—It is to be observed, that the Carbonari have adopted names, some ancient, some modern, but all differing from those in common use, for the districts where they have

1818. "All the Carbonari of the Western Lucanian Republic have the natural and inalienable right of adoring the Almighty according to the dictates of their own understanding and conscience."[16] This is of course one motive of the rooted aversion of the Popes to this order.

But, though such free toleration is allowed, the ceremonies of admission partake of an almost fanatic superstition. The novices were told that, in imitation of their Grand Master, Christ, they must necessarily pass through sufferings to purity and happiness; they were crowned with thorns,[17] and a reed was placed in their hands. A dramatic representation exhibited part of the agonies of the Saviour, and it was solemnly announced, that the great requisites were to preserve their faith, and mutually to assist each other.

The following extract from the 1st. chap. of the statutes of Carbonarism will tend to explain the real or pretended principles of the sect.

Of the General Doctrine of the Order

Art. 1. Good Cousinship is principally founded on religion and virtue.

Art. 2. The place of meeting is called the Barac-

---

established their lodge.

16   Cap. 2. Art. 8. Delia Esposizione dei Dritti dei Carbonari della Republica Lucana Occidentale.

17   See App. III. for the ceremonies of initiation.

ca; the space surrounding it, the Forest or Wood; the interior of the Lodge, the Vendita.

Art. 3. The Members are called Good Cousins; they are divided into two classes—Apprentices and Masters.

Art. 4. Tried virtue and purity of morals, and not Pagan[18] qualities, render men worthy of belonging to the Carbonari.

Art. 5. An interval of six months is necessary before an apprentice can obtain the rank of Master. The principal obligations imposed on him are, to practise benevolence, to succour the unfortunate, to show docility of mind, to bear no malice against Carbonari, and to enrich his heart with virtue.

Art. 6. By this article it is forbidden to talk directly or indirectly against religion, and by

Art. 7. All conversation on religion in general, or against good morals, is prohibited.

Art. 8. Every Good Cousin Carbonaro is obliged to preserve inviolable secrecy concerning the mysteries of the Order.

Art. 9. No G. C. C. may communicate what is done or decided upon in his Vendita, to those who belong to another, much less to persons not initiated.

Art. 10. The greatest reserve is recommended to the Members, towards all persons with whom they are not well acquainted, but more especially in the bosoms of their own families.

---

18   Pagan. Pagano may be translated profane, belonging to the uninitiated.

* * *

The centre of the machinations of the Carbonari was formed in the capital itself, and was intended to be permanently established there, as affording the most effectual means of concealment. The Alta Vendita, or principal lodge, was composed of honorary members and of deputies from each particular Vendita. It was declared to be an administrative and legislative body, a court of council and of appeal; and it was accordingly divided into different sections. It was the business of this Vendita to grant charters of organization to new lodges, or to confirm such as were submitted for its approbation. It has continued to retain its powers, but was eclipsed, before the revolution of 1820, by the superior activity and influence of the Carbonari magistracy of the Western Lucanian Republic[19] The Diet of the Carbonari of that district doubted and debated whether it should acknowledge the Alta Vendita, or General Assembly of the capital, which met provisionally, after the revolution, in the Convent of San Domenico Grande, and referred the decision to a committee, who were of opinion that two deputies from each tribe[20] should be sent thither in order to organize a real general assembly of the Carbonari; to which, however, it was not thought expedient to

19   Western Lucania is the Carbonaro name for the province of Principato Citra.

20   The subdivisions of the Carbonari are called tribes.

1. Place of the Grand Master. 2. Place of the Apprentinces. 3 Grand Master 4. Orator. 5. Secretary. 6. The Adept. 7. Master of the Ceremonies. 8 & 9. 1st and 2nd Assistants. 10. Picture of St Theobald.

grant the power assumed by the old Assembly, of dictating laws peremptorily.

The committee further suggested, that if the Alta Vendita could not be prevailed upon to meet this plan, the same deputies should be authorized to negotiate with the Vendite of other provinces, and especially with the Republics of Hirpinia, Daunia, Picentia, Eastern Lucania, Lecce, Cosenza, and Catanzaro, to extend the league; and to establish a central assembly of the confederate provinces. It will appear, in the sequel, that Salerno has superseded Naples as the head-quarters of the Carbonari. We must now return to the circumstances of the infant institution.

The description of the Vendita, extracted from the Code of Carbonarism,[21] will assist the reader to comprehend the explanations of the symbols, painted on the patents of the initiated, and used at their meetnigs.

Of the Decorations of the Vendita of the First Rank

The Vendita will be represented by a room of planks covered also with wood.

The pavement must be of brick; the interior furnished with seats without backs. At the end there must be a block supported by three legs (*basi*); on the two sides there must be two other blocks

---

21   Sect. 1.

of the same size, for the assistants. On the block of the Grand Master there must be the following symbols: a linen cloth; water; salt; a cross; leaves; sticks; fire; earth; a crown of white thorns; a ladder; a ball of thread, and three ribbons, one blue, one red, and one black. There must be an illuminated (*raggiante*) triangle, with the initial letters of the pass-word of the second rank in the middle. On the left hand there must be a triangle, with the arms of the Vendita painted. On the right three triangles, each with the initial letters of the sacred words of the first rank. The triangles should be transparent; that is to say, with the light behind.

On the admission of apprentices, the symbolical picture of the Vendita, and the emblems on the patents, which are a repetition of it, were explained after a discourse on the natural liberty of man, its forfeiture by the perverseness of the wicked, and the necessity for recovering it by the efforts of the Society.

The initiated were addressed more openly as soon as they had shown an aptitude for seizing allegories, or when they belonged to a more enlightened class of society.

The two following initiatory discourses present a striking contrast to each other. The first, extracted from the Constitution of the order at Naples, is calculated for uncultivated persons. The second was found among the papers of the Roman Conspirators of 1817; among whom were many persons of birth and education.

First Discourse, Pronounced
by the Grand Master

"Hear me, dear and good Cousins:

"Nature, when she created man, meant him to be free. It is, therefore, the duty of every man to keep himself so, and to fulfil the engagement she has imposed on him by diffusing liberty among his brethren, by communicating his pleasures to them, by partaking in their pains and labours, and by considering himself on an equality with all his fellow creatures, so that he may exalt himself to the most sublime heights of virtue.

Unfortunately, the flattering hopes of seeing such virtue become universal have been deceived. The tender name of brother has been renounced; and man has treated his fellow-man as an enemy. At first the strong usurped the rights of the weak. Afterwards violence was superseded by cunning. Hence arose intrigue, hatred, treason, imposture, superstition: man became the vile slave of his infamous passions. Yet Reason, sovereign of the human mind, enlightened some sager individuals as to the real nature of things. She preserved them from the general corruption; and they endeavoured to bring back their wandering fellow mortals to the neglected paths of virtue. But, deaf to the voice of reason, they rejected her precepts. It was then that, still indefatigable, those benevolent sages conceived the idea of secret societies, which, assiduously labouring to give a better education to mankind, might be the means of exciting them to virtue; and these societies are those of the Carbonari."

Explanation of the Symbols According to the Neapolitan Constitution

1. The trunk of the tree which you see, expresses the surface of the earth on which the Good Cousins are dispersed. It denotes also the firmament equally spread above all; and shows us that our wants are equal, and our interests the same. The roots of the tree mark its stability. Its verdant foliage, and the strength by which it resists the storm, indicate that it never grows old; and that as our first parents, after having lost their innocence, covered their shame with leaves, the Good Cousins ought to conceal the faults of their fellow men, and particularly those of the Society.

2. The white linen on which you have been received, is the produce of a plant. By maceration and by labour it is become such as you see it; so ought we to purify and cleanse ourselves by continual efforts. Enveloped in linen when the natural light first shone upon us, it receives us again at the moment of our regeneration to virtue.

3. Water cleansed us when we came from the womb; it teaches us here to purify ourselves from the stains of vice, in order that, being delivered from its contamination, we may enjoy the pleasures of virtue.

4. Salt, the means of preserving corruptible things, exhorts us to preserve our hearts from the general corruption.

5. The crown of white thorns placed upon our heads reminds us to be cautious and steady in our movements and actions, to avoid the pain of being wounded.

6. The cross foreshows the labours, the persecutions, the death that threatens those who aspire to virtue. It exhorts us to persevere in imitating the example of Jesus Christ, our Grand Master, who willingly suffered death to bring us nearer to salvation.

7. The earth buries the body in eternal oblivion; and it is thus that the secret of our sacred order should be buried in the bottom of our hearts. It is the most important symbol of our institution. The Pagans spread snares for us; they are perverse enough to mistrust our associations, the very instruments of their redemption and happiness. And were they to penetrate our secret, they might force us to sustain an unequal combat.

8. The ladder shows the G. C. C. that virtue is only to be attained step by step.

9. The bundles of sticks denote the members of our respectable order, united in peace.

10. The ribbons, the principal decoration of the Carbonari, express by their colours the cardinal virtues. Black, or the charcoal, is faith. Blue, or the smoke of our august furnace, is hope: and red, or the fire, charity.

11. The specimen of wood,[22] which is the appropriate badge of the apprentices, is to be fastened to their coats at the button-hole by a tri-coloured ribbon. Several of similar shapes are stuck into the ground at regular distances, to mark the dwellings of Good Cousins. Its form is that of the pole of the furnace of real charcoal burners; the extremities are cut diagonally. The masters wear a badge of the same form in silver.

12. The thread of that ball is the mysterious tie which unites us.

13. The axe, the mattock, and the shovel, are the tools of our sacred labours, &c.

"The President marks the signals, and orders (*vantaggi*) by a stroke of his axe on the block before him."

Discourse extracted from the Papers Found upon the Conspirators of Macerata, 1817.[23]

"The earliest societies of men, hoping to find happiness within the walls of cities, entrusted the command of their forces to one person for the common defence. He, instead of protecting and defending them, became their oppressor. Civil equality disappeared; and the rights of man were dethroned

---

22 The specimen of wood refers to the sample offered by the wood-cutters to their customers.

23 Printed Minutes of the Trial Rome, 1818.

by despotism. Corrupted human nature suffered the laws of truth and justice to be supplanted by depravity of manners, and by the persecution and oppression of the good.

"A few wise and good men who still cherished in their hearts that morality, whose principles are unalterable, either by change of time or the succession of generations, while they wept over these evils in secret, ruminated on the means of preserving untainted some sentiment of sound morality. They secretly imparted their knowledge and their views to a few persons worthy of the distinction. Thus transmitted from generation to generation, their maxims became the fountain of that true philosophy which can never be corrupted nor altered in its appearance. It is in the school founded on them that, without veil or mystery, men are taught to respect and to maintain the rights of their fellow men.

"The mysteries of Mythras in Persia, of Isis in Egypt, of Eleusis in Greece, and of the temples yet to be rebuilt, and the light that is yet to be spread,[24] are all so many rays proceeding from the same centre, moving in an orbit whose field is the immensity of wisdom.

"Carbonarism is not the last or least of the societies that have proceeded from this school. It has simplified many various systems, and adopted only the unaffected language of nature. It presents

---

24   Ed i Templi da riedificarsi, e la Luce da stendersi,

itself without mystery to those who know how to understand it; it receives them into its peaceful bosom, and elevates them to the contemplation of never varying nature, to the love of man collectively, to the hatred of oppression and despotism, to the knowledge of good, and of all that is useful to society, and confirms the general systems of truth and justice.

"Carbonarism teaches in its baracche the true end of moral existence, and gives rules of conduct for social life. It points out the means for diffusing the light of truth, and for disseminating the principles of philosophy and equality. It is to the sacred rights of equality that the G. C. must especially attach himself."

Explanation of the Symbols

"The cross should serve to crucify the tyrant who persecutes us, and troubles our sacred operations. The crown of thorns should serve to pierce his head. The thread denotes the cord to lead him to the gibbet; the ladder will aid him to mount. The leaves are nails to pierce his hands and feet. The pick-axe will penetrate his breast, and shed the impure blood that flows in his veins. The axe will separate his head from his body, as the wolf who disturbs our pacific labours. The salt will prevent the corruption of his head, that it may last as a monument of the eternal infamy of despots.

The pole will serve to put the skull of the tyrant upon. The furnace will burn his body. The shovel will scatter his ashes to the wind. The baracca will serve to prepare new tortures for the tyrant. The fountain will purify us from the vile blood we shall have shed. The linen will wipe away our stains, and render us clean and pure. The forest is the place where the Good Cousins labour to obtain so important a result. The trunk with a single branch signifies that, after the great operation, we shall become equal to the N. C."

* * *

One would be tempted to doubt the reality of the last explanation of the symbols, if it were not given in the minutes of a legal trial. Perhaps the compiler of the notes may have confounded the verbal depositions of some of the witnesses with what he thought he had read in the catechisms of the sect.

Although the general doctrine of the order makes mention but of two ranks of Carbonari, a single pamphlet of eight pages, without a title or the name of the publisher, which has fallen into the author's hands, makes mention of a third, and describes its operations and the mode of initiation.[25] The object of this third rank or order is to procure information concerning the signs and sacred words known and understood by men of different

___

25 Travagli del 3ro Grado. The style is contemptible; and the sense for the most part, must be guessed at.

nations on the whole surface of the globe towards east and west, towards mid-day and midnight. The Vendita represents a cavern in the interior of a mountain. In one corner is seen a rustic urn, with this inscription, "Here he's the hero." The absurd story of this heroic personage is related to the new member immediately after his initiation in these words:—

"Philip the Macedonian, having undertaken to conquer the great city of Thebes in Beotia with a powerful army, was resisted by the brave citizens on the borders of their territory with all the force they could muster, animated by the resolution to save their country or to die, and by having for their general the great Philomel, a citizen celebrated for his good qualities. Unfortunately, in spite of their courage, they were overcome, broken and dispersed. The great warrior Philomel, remaining, together with a few brave citizens, sought by every means in his power to be revenged on Philip; but, before he made his attack, finding that some das-tardly Thebans had declared for the Macedonians, and courted their own chains, the great Philomel invented the expedient of concealing his heroes by communicating to them conventional signs and words. They attacked the tyrant a second time, but with even less success than before, and were broken and defeated. Philomel, seeing his belov-ed country in the power of Philip, sought a glo-rious death by precipitating himself from a high rock, and died as bravely as he had lived. Before his death he advised his friends to keep their signs and words secret; and exhorted them to increase their numbers, and to spread themselves over the whole earth, with the determination of making war against tyranny, false opinion, and prejudice. After this discourse the Grand Master explains the signs, and communicates the sacred words."[26]

The other secret sects profess equally to have the independence of their country solely in view. In the catechism of the Guelphs, "Italy, torn and oppressed," is indicated by the mystic name of

---

26 *Filippo il Macedono, avendo, con un poderoso esercito, intrapreso a soggrocare (soggiogare) la gran città di Tebbe (Tebe) in Boezia (Beozia), fu da' valorosi cittadini di questi contrade ai confini del loro territorio con tutta la forza che poterono radunare (combatuto ?) animati pero dal deciso sentimento, o di salvare la patria, o di morire, e l'essere per loro Duce il Gran Filomelo, cittadino cognito per le sue virtù —la disgrazia voile che ad onta del loro coraggio, furono oppressi, rotti, e sbarragliati; il gran guerriero Filomelo essendo rimasto con altri bravi cittadini circo per quanto pote di fare conoscere a (contro) Filippo le sue mire; ma prima di portarsi all' attacco vedendo che alcuni vili Tebbani si erano dichiarati della parte de' Macedoni e che cercavano colle loro mani delle ritorte, il Gran Filomelo penso accio non si conoscessero gli Eroi di communicargli dei segni e parole: ed attaccando la seconda volta il tiranno, ma con più infelice successo della prima, forono rotti e vinti. Vedendo Filomelo la sua cara patria in potere di Filippo andiede a darsi una morte gloriosa precipitandosi da un alta rupe et fini da prode qual visse i giorni suoi, inculcando prima di morire agli amici di tenere celati il segni e la parola, e che si aumentassero, e spargessero per tutto il globo terreno, e di essere decisi di fare la guerra alia tirannia, alia falsa opinione, ed al pregiudizio.*

Ed inde il Gran Maestro li communicherk i segni e la parola sagra, &c

mother. These sectaries, who call themselves her children, declare themselves bound and resolved to succour and to comfort her. They assert boldly that the moment of her resuscitation is at hand, *when the cock shall crow afresh; when the eagles shall fight; when the bulls shall wrestle; when the harp shall provoke the dolphms; when the moon shall be covered with blood; and the bark shall remain aground*; a metaphorical prophecy concerning persons and nations, and a new war which is to overturn the present governments of Italy. At the time when these societies were formed, the public mind was singularly prepared to receive with avidity all that could excite and elevate the imagination. Men's minds seemed to be possessed anew with the enthusiasm of the twelfth century,[27] when the liberties of the Italian cities and republics were founded amidst the struggles between the Emperors and the Popes, and on the ruins of the authority of the former.

"It was then," observes an historian of distinguished merit,[28] in relating the wars of Frederick Barbarossa against Alexander III., "that men began to make use of those mystical representations of religion which had been preserved from time immemorial in the valleys of the Alps, the seat of ancient modes of thinking, which had their origin in Switzerland, the Pays de Vaud, the villages of the

---

27 1159–1162.
28 Johannes Von Mlilleiv, Allgeraeiner Geschichten. B. xv. Kap. 5

Valais and of the Cevennes. Their characteristics were, the simplicity, the freedom, and the equality of the first Christian communities. But some Gnostic prejudices against social order had gradually led to an exaggerated system of morals. Could it be supposed that the Emperor would make use of these men against Rome? far from it: he joined the Church against them; their ideas of liberty did not coincide with his plan of government, which was formed on that of the Cæsars, He had caused Arnold de Brescia, the most enterprising agent of the sectaries, to be burnt for favouring the attempt made by the nobility to procure the freedom of Rome by the assistance of the people. The spirit of Arnold remained, and mingled with the rising liberties of the free bughers."

The error of creating a state within a state, and of erecting secret tribunals to redress wrongs, has existed in all barbarous and turbulent times, It is of very ancient date in the kingdom of the two Sicilies. About the period to which we have just alluded, that is 1186, under William II. the Norman, according to the Chronicles of the Abbeys of Fossa Nuova and of Monte Casino, a sect of presumptuous men, devanis hominibus, arose. They took the name of avengers, *Vendicosi*, and did all the mischief in their power, not by day, but by night. At length Adiorolphus, of Ponte Corvo, Grand Master of the sect, was hanged by order of the King, and many of his partisans branded with a hot iron.

The members of a second Sicilian Society, almost unknown to the rest of Europe, called themselves the Beati Paoli. Their actions and their motives perfectly resembled those of the Free Knights[29] in Germany. Persons of all ranks united themselves secretly, and proceeded especially against the great barons and the tribunals, whose power was such that they were not to be reached openly.

This institution, vicious and horrible in itself, did, however, produce some partially salutary effects, restraining the arbitrary licentiousness of the great, by the terror with which it inspired them. The punishments inflicted by the Beati Paoli were death by poison or the dagger, mutilation, destruction of property by fire, and for the slightest crimes or faults, the severest beating. The ramifications of this Society were spread over the whole island. The most formidable companies were those of Messina and Trapani. It is said that papers relating to the Society still exist in the archives of the two cities; and though it was most powerful in the middle ages, traces of its existence are to be found as late as the eighteenth century. A cavern is shown at Palermo, in a street called de Canceddi, near the church of Santa Maria di Gesu, where they held their meetings, and the grandfather of the present Prince of Trabia caused one of their most daring chieftains, surnamed Testa Longa, to be executed.

---

29   Die Vehingericlite.

It was in vain that the government published the severest laws, and denounced the heaviest penalties against them in all the pragmatic acts of the kingdom; but the change in the state of society, and the improvement of manners, at length put an end to the association. A lively recollection of it still, however, remains among the Sicilians; and they are heard to exclaim, on receiving any injury or loss, for which they cannot apply to justice, "*Ah, se fossero ancora i Beati Paoli!*" Ah, if the Beati Paoli were still in being!

The Carbonari have adopted some of the forms of the Beati Paoli. If any unfortunate being has incurred their vengeance, especially if it be by any act of infidelity towards the sect, the Grand Masters meet in what is called a chamber of honour, and deliberate on his fate. If he be condemned, they write his name on a piece of paper, which is burnt, and he is registered in the Black Book with those, who, having presented themselves as candidates for admission into the Society, have been rejected as unworthy.[30] The sentence is executed

---

30   "The *Black Book* is that in which the Christian and surnames, the age, the country, and the condition of all the Pagans who have been unsuccessful candidates for Carbonarism, are inscribed. The Vendita which rejected them, and the number of votes against them, must also be entered. The Good Cousins whose names have been burnt, the usual punishment for betraying the secrets of the order, by any particular Vendita, or even by the Alta Vendita itself, must be registered in the same book, and the rank they held in the society is to be noted. The *Golden Book* is the register of the regulations, elections, and installations of officers of the order. It contains besides a list

by whoever is especially named for the purpose, and the rest of the lodge cannot resist or annul it. Although the printed penal statute of the Western Lucanian Republic makes no explicit mention of the punishment of death, yet it contains some articles which clearly imply it. The punishments are divided under the heads of degradation and penalties in general. The first head is again subdivided into

1st. Devoting to general execration.

2d. Burning the name, or the person in effigy.

3d. Unanimous black-balling—*anneramento*.[31]

Among the consequences of these punishments, are interdiction of water and fire, the prohibition of all communication between other Good Cousins and the criminal, whose name, written in large letters, is affixed in all the vendite, and read at every sitting. "The *Anneramento*," they observe, may be effaced by time, but " infamy attaches itself for ever."

The execration is more than mere disapprobation. Its mystery is explained in the 55th article of the 9th section, "On Crimes against Individuals," which declares that a murderer is not punishable, when the person put to death is a Carbonaro, condemned, after trial, to general execration, or to

---

of all the regular Vendite, and such debates as are of general importance to the society." See *Constitution of the Order of Good Cousins at Naples*, section 10 of the Archives.

31 *Anneramento*, the consequence of black-balling, *i. e.* being inscribed in the *Black Book*.

have his name or effigy burnt. The oath of initiation itself is a proof that the punishment of death is among the engines used by this dangerous society.

Excepting in the case of the absolute power exercised by the vendite, the Secret Societies flatter the predominating taste of the age for equality. The rich and the poor, the noble and the artisan, are here confounded. The same charm had attracted thousands of converts to the bosom of the infant Christian church. The Agapæ, the Communion, and the Catacombs, placed the slave on a footing with his master. The priesthood, being accessible to all, levelled all. And this equality reconciled the lower order of proselytes to the privations and dangers to which they were perpetually exposed. The Roman Emperors perceived the danger. They put the existing prohibitory laws against secret meetings in force against the Christians. Trajan published no new edict against their dogmas, but he forbade their meetings as contrary to the welfare of the Republic, and of religion.[32] It was in consequence of this decree, that the Pagan magistrates introduced themselves among the Christians, who, under cover of night, offered up their prayers and praises to God; and punished them tyrannically as forming a college, or fellowship, sodalitium, apart in the state, and belonging to a dissenting religion, whose chief was the Pope, or Bishop of Rome.[33]

---

32   Pliny, the Pro-Consul in Bithynia, writes to Trajan, that the order to that effect had been published.

33   St. Clement, who was first exiled and afterwards received the

The Carbonari are called a sect, a name which seems to imply a religious distinction in Italy; and the appellation does not displease them.

It is curious to listen to the fanatics of the Society, while they detail the miraculous conversions which it has already wrought. The ferocious Lazzaroni of Naples, and the wildest brigands of the Calabrias and the Abruzzi have been known, immediately on their initiation, to perform the most striking acts of benevolence and justice. Under this pretext, of bringing back the wicked to the ways of virtue, distinguished brigand chiefs are admitted into the order. The notorious Gaetano Vardarelli himself was a Carbonaro."[34]

---

crown of martyrdom.—*Baronius ad Ann. Christi* 100.

34 The Revolution at Naples has not diminished this sympathy for malefactors, although their alliance is no longer of such importance as at first. Repeated proposals have been made to set the least notorious at liberty, in order to form them into armed companies; and the legislative assembly has deigned to take these proposals into consideration.

"All the prisons are filled with convicts," says the famous address to the national Parliament, drawn up in pursuance of an order issued by the Alta Vendita, by its Grand Master, Giuliano, in the month of October, 1820.[a] "There are some among them whom misery has driven to crime. Rome has more than once armed her slaves, and Sparta has employed her helots, after having set them at liberty. Select from these prisoners such as are not guilty of the worst crimes, and form a free corps of them. They will enter upon a new course of life, and may be rendered useful to themselves and to the country, which will at the same time be freed from a burden."

a   Indrizzo al P. N. (*Parlamento Naazionale*) presso Pasquali Tezzano, strada Cisterna dell' Olio, No. 26. This address was Avithdrawn from circulation, and is

So far is this system carried, that an assassin, condemned to the chain, is permitted to take his place in the Vendita of the Castle of St. Elmo, where he is confined with other galley-slaves, and the commander of the fort, himself a Carbonaro, has not dared to exclude him, but is obliged to sit by his side. The Carbonari, like the English Puritans during the Civil Wars, affect great austerity of manners, and talk of reformation. They cause such Good Cousins as have committed excesses to do public penance in the Vendite. They preach against games of chance, and it is at their instigation, that such games have been prohibited. Their oath contains a clause, by which they are bound to respect the conjugal honour, and the good name of the Carbonari. And praiseworthy actions are reported at their meetings, and registered.[35]

---

now difficult to procure.

35 For example.—Art. 31. of the proceedings of the second sitthig of the Grand Diet of Salerno, (August 20, 1820.)—"The Good Cousin Gatti, who was seized and wounded on the 21st of the 9th month (June), by the Good Cousin F. Copeta, renews the generous act of pardoning him, and invites all the Good Cousins to follow his example." The Grand Diet decides that this "virtuous act be published, and printed, and communicated to all the Vendite of the Republic," &c., and in the proceedings of the 4th sitting of this Diet, the same fact is again alluded to *Art.* 57. " It has been debated, whether the person named Copeta, who seized and wounded the Good Cousin Gatti, ought to profit by the pardon of the latter. It has been determined, that the generosity of Gatti is not sufficient to retain Copeta in the family of the Carbonari, but only to preserve him from severer punishment; and it has therefore been decided to burp his name, i. e. to expel him from the Society.

It is the office of the magistracy or senate to watch over the conduct of the citizens of the Republic. And its satisfaction or displeasure is signified by such public notices as the following:

*"From the Central District of Salerno,
16th of the 11th month, 3d year.*

"The Magistracy exercising the executive power of the Western Lucanian Republic,[36] to the Councils of the Tribes, and all the Vendite of the said Republic.[37]

"The magistracy has hitherto been well satisfied with the good conduct of the Carbonari, but some unpleasant representations have lately been made. It is said, that private revenge pollutes the virtue of some Good Cousins; that discord and dissension divide our families; that ambition has shown itself, to the disgrace of the moderation of our order, *della Carbonica moderazione*; that the abuse of arms, which are now needless, has increased beyond measure, that the public authorities are despised, and that the property of the Commons and the Royal demesnes are invaded. The magistracy cannot believe that all this can be true. But if it be so, why, Good Cousins, why throw discredit on us? Why be our own enemies? Why subject ourselves

---

36   The province of Principato citra.

37   The tribes are the Pecentina, the Pestana, the Consilina, the Velina.

to hatred, instead of securing the love of the nation? Why disgrace a cause, which has hitherto reflected so much honour and so much glory on the Carbonari? Let the Grand Masters therefore be on the watch to admonish with paternal tenderness, and where that will not suffice, let the orators be ready to bring to trial, and to punishment, such offenders as shall be found obdurate. The magistracy has published an advertisement, and directs that the same be circulated throughout the Republic.

Advertisement

For some days, private offences, quarrels, and vexations have been frequent, and the enemies of good order would fain attribute them to the Carbonari. They are certainly not capable of such conduct, having hitherto given most sufficient proofs to the contrary; but if any Good Cousin should be guilty of the slightest of these misdemeanours, let the aggrieved party repair to the authorities, in full confidence of immediate redress. He who cannot command his own passions is unworthy of the name of Carbonaro."[38]

---

38   In the month of October, 1820, robbery, accompanied with violence and housebreaking, had increased to so great a degree at Naples, that the Minister of Justice, Ricciardi, proposed to the Parliament to suspend the liberty of the individual, in order to arrest those suspected of such outrages. As public rumour principally accused the armed Carbonari of these crimes, the provisional assembly of the order thought it expedient to pub-

The penal statutes of the Western Lucanian Republic, to which we have already referred, contain some laws on general conduct, an extract from which may not be uninteresting. They are so austere, that no ordinary legislator would have ventured to impose them. It would have been almost impossible to enforce a strict observance of them while the sect was still under the restraint of absolute secrecy, and, consequently, even the masters of the Vendite subject to mutual opposition. But the importance of such laws at the present moment will be easily conceived, when we find that the most uneducated part of the Neapolitan population, that part which has been hitherto destitute of all moral principle, is united into one society, without much distinction or inquiry.

Penal Statutes, Sect. 4th.—Offences[39]
against Public Order

Art. 24. Whoever shall be habitually intimate with persons degraded in the eyes of the public, shall be punished by suspension from all participation in the sacred labours, for a period of from two months to a year.

Art. 25. Whoever gambles for wine, or frequents public-houses, or who shall appear often in public

---

lish the proclamation, which forms No. VII. of the Appendix.

39 Talli.—Act. 2. Preliminary Regulations. "All transgressions against the laws of the Carbonari are called Falli."

in a state of intoxication, shall be punished by suspension as above.

Art. 26. Those who break the social tie, by abandoning their families to want, and who give themselves to a dissolute life, shall be suspended for a period of from six months to two years.

Art. 27. Those who play at games of chance among themselves shall undergo the same punishment for the same space of time.

Section 10th.—Offences against Honour

Art. 65. Whoever shall attempt the honour of females, belonging to Good Cousins, shall be punished by being given up to general execration.

Art. 66. By females belonging to Good Cousins, are to be understood, 1st, wives, daughters, mothers, sisters, and all female relations to the second degree; 2d, females devoted to the exclusive attachment of Good Cousins are included in this class; 3d, female relations in whatsoever degree, residing with Good Cousins, are also to be understood.

Art. 67. Any attempt at violence subjects the offender to the punishment of execration.

Art. 68. Those who do not resist the criminal invitations of the wives of Good Cousins shall have their names inserted in the Black Book, anneramento.

Art. 69. Those who lend themselves to the failings of their family, whether wives, sisters, cousins, or persons otherwise related, shall undergo the same punishment.

Art. 70. Such persons as shall take advantage of the weakness of degraded females, shall be suspended from the society, for a period of from six months to two years.

Art. 73. Good Cousins who are married are forbidden to have other attachments, under pain of being suspended from the society, during a period of from two to six years.

Art. 74. Those who shall seduce or carry off the female servants of Good Cousins, for base purposes, shall be suspended for a term of from one to three years.

The same crimes are punished much less severely when Pagans and their wives are the plaintiffs; the proportion is as one to ten, as we learn from Articles 71 and 72.[40] So that it is not morality itself which these Lycurguses have at heart, but the prevention of jealousies and division among the members of the order.

No society, intended by its founders to be so widely spread, ever sought to detach its members so completely from the state, by imposing on them a legislation distinct in its form, and at variance with its laws. It seems as if the progress of the cler-

---

40   *Art.* 71. Violence offered to the wives of Pagans constitutes an offence punishable by Anneramento, being inscribed in the black book.

      Art. 72. Those who shall seduce the female relations of respectable Pagans shall be suspended from the society for a period of from two to six months.

gy in the Middle Ages, and their pretensions to be independent on temporal tribunals, had served the Carbonari as a model. The Good Cousins are strictly forbidden to refer their causes to the ordinary judges until they have reported them to one belonging to the sect. In the statutes of the Western Lucanian Republic, the only cases in which it is allowable to infringe the rule, are laid down. The institution of juries is solemnly adopted by the Carbonari.

Art. 22. "In criminal prosecutions the Carbonari of the Western Lucanian Republic have a right to be heard by counsel, and to know the cause and nature of the accusations brought against them. They have also a right to confront witnesses, to bring forward evidence in their own favour, and to demand a speedy and public trial by means of an impartial jury, without whose verdict they cannot be pronounced guilty. No man can be deprived of his rights, and the judgment of his peers, but by the laws of the republic.

Art. 23. "The institution of juries shall be resorted to in the investigation of any controversy whatever that may arise among the Carbonari of Western Lucania.

Art. 24. "The Carbonari of the Western Lucanian district have a right to bring forward their respective complaints, of what nature soever, in the assemblies of the Carbonari; but no one may lodge complaints against his Good Cousin in the Pagan tribunals, except in the following cases:—

1. "When the complaints have not been attended to by the Carbonari.

2. "When, after the sentence of the Order, the assembly by which it has been passed may have reasons for permitting a further investigation in a Pagan court."

It certainly augurs but ill for the new constitutional government of Naples, and proves how little confidence is reposed in it, that the Carbonari not only continue to follow the same system of judicial separation, but have lately made some alterations and additions in their code, which show that they intend to persevere. The grand diet of Salerno, for instance, *Art.* 63, at the meeting of the 3d of August, 1820, decrees,

> That the Grand Diet, in consequence of the happy change of circumstances, considers a revision of the present laws of the order to be indispensable. It therefore appoints a committee, composed of the Good Cousins Rossi, Giuseppe Nicola, Caviglia Giacomo, and Farina Giacinto, to take them into consideration. A deputation of sixteen deputies, four from each tribe, shall, for the present, ratify their opinion in the name of the people; and the laws so reformed shall be put in force until a further decision of the Grand Diet of the next year.

The committee having given in their report, it was printed in three parts, each of which was ratified by the Diet under the following titles.

Organization of the Judicial Authority

The representatives of the Carbonari of the Western Lucanian Republic, at a meeting of the Grand Diet of the year, perceiving the necessity of establishing a constant system of regulation for the judicial proceedings of the Order, have sanctioned, and do sanction the following act, which distributes and defines the functions of judicial power,

&c. &c.

Code of Judicial Proceedings

" The representatives of the Carbonari, &c. have sanctioned, and do sanction the following act, which distributes and fixes the regulations to be observed by witnesses, juries," &c.

Penal Statutes

"The representatives of the Carbonari, &c. perceiving the necessity of establishing a regular system of punishment for offences of which the Carbonari may be guilty, have sanctioned, and do sanction," &c. &c.

A decree of the Western Lucanian Republic enacts, that

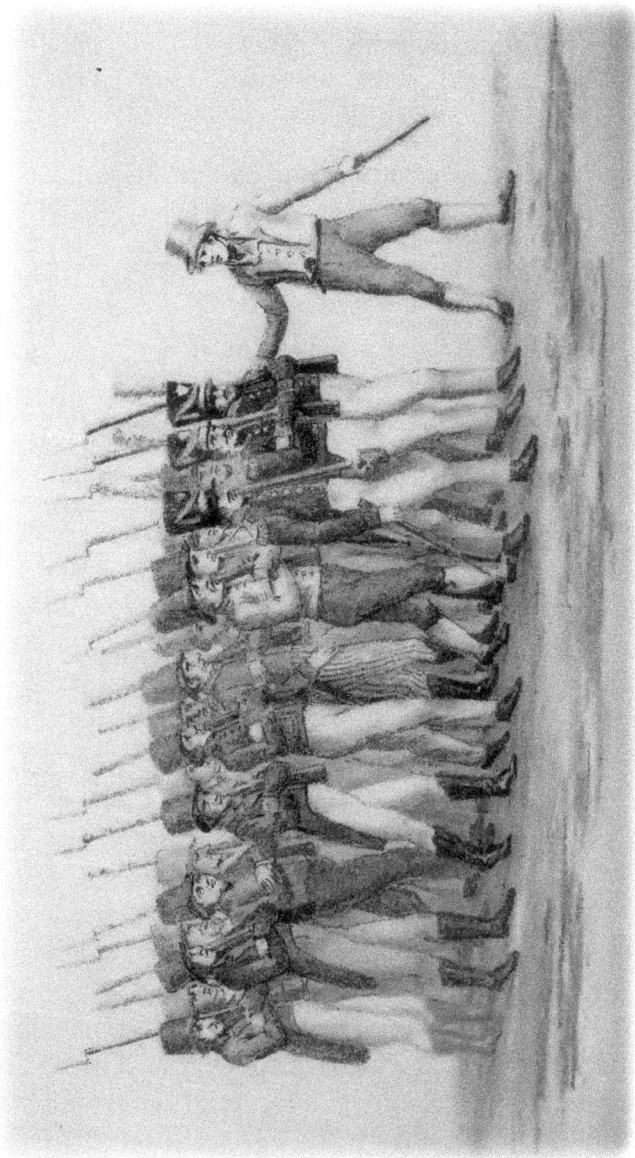

Carbonaro Patrol Commanded by a Police Officer, Himself a Carbonaro

as the Carbonari of the Republic must preserve a military attitude until the constitutional government is really consolidated, they are all required to be in arms, to maintain the imprescriptible rights of the nation, and to ensure the constitution and Royal family against all hostile attempts.

Again, *Art.* 14.

exact registers should be kept, in which the names of such as come forward willingly shall be entered as honourable and brave—*Onorati e prodi*; —while such as refuse to march, unless they be lame, or otherwise physically incapable, shall be stigmatized as without honour, and cowards, *senza onore e codardi.*

These regulations have enabled the magistracies of the Carbonari to contribute powerfully to cause young recruits and soldiers on furlow to join their different corps, and to prevent desertion in the interior.

In the capital the patrols of Carbonari preserve good order, parading the streets night and day, headed by constables and agents of police, whom they have forced to be initiated, in order to become worthy of the command; and they are now organizing a Carbonaro guard of safety, *Guardia di sicurezza Carbonara*, dressed in a particular uniform, of which we give a specimen. It will be remarked, that one of the characteristic ornaments is the death's head on the cartouch box. It is ev-

Guard of the Carbonaro Legion

ident, that the troops acting from this impulse, though its direction is, for the moment, in favour of government, are too little under its controul, not to be able to turn against it so soon as the Vendite, which are in fact political debating clubs, shall receive orders from their superiors to that effect. The truth is, that the executive power of the state is in their hands; and it rests with them alone to disband the regular troops, the soldiers of which, being Carbonari, do not obey their officers from any principle of military discipline, but solely because it is the will of the society.

The number of Carbonari has increased with astonishing rapidity. They amounted to from twenty-four to thirty thousand from the very beginning of their establishment. The whole population of some towns in the Abruzzi and the Calabrias enlisted themselves. Lanciano, for instance, though an inconsiderable place, had 1200 men armed in 1814.

Admission to the first rank of Carbonarism is easily obtained; and whoever objects to going through the ceremony in the grand assembly, may perform it before three Grand Masters in private. As nothing was trusted to the apprentices, nothing was risked by multiplying them. The main object was to secure a number of satellites, ready to obey invisible superiors, and directions which they cannot understand.

The magistrates, as well as the civil and military officers, have been often obliged to become members of the society, in order to preserve some shadow of their authority. But the lower clergy enrolled themselves of their own free will; and seconded the views of the institution by every means in their power. The number of priests initiated, notwithstanding the severest prohibitions pronounced by the Holy See, is a proof that the Roman hierarchy, like all other ancient institutions, is in danger from its own members. The lower clergy form the democratic and revolutionary part of the society; immense numbers of them have taken part openly in the late troubles; among whom Menechini at Nola, and Guida at Salerno, have distinguished themselves. Thirty priests are named in the official reports concerning the insurgents at Benevento; some monks were the first to exasperate the populace of Palermo against the Neapolitan troops; and the Jesuits first instigated the declaration of Sicilian independence at Girgenti. The greater number of those priests who, after the temporary abandonment of their convents, caused by the events of the French Revolution, had been forced to re-assume the religious habit either by their own wants, or by the orders of their superiors, felt nothing but the privations and restraints to which they had ceased to be accustomed within the walls of the cloister; and they were no longer consoled for these privations by the veneration with which they had formerly been regarded without its precincts. Many of the curates and poor priests sigh for promotion by seniority, as it is regulated in the army, and look upon young prelates of rank, as the soldiers and officers of Bonaparte do upon the noblemen placed at the head of their companies without having served in the campaigns. They maintain that the Pope and the bishops are the usurpers of their rights; that the primitive church had opened the priesthood to all without respect of persons; and they hold themselves beyond the reach of the anathemae thundered against the Carbonari, because they are pronounced by the Holy Father, who is a party as well as judge in the cause.

The lower priests at Naples contend that the laws of the kingdom ratify the edicts of the Pope only when accompanied by the "Exequatur" of the king, which was never added to the edict condemning the Carbonari. They therefore replied by a remonstrance to Pope Pius VII. which will be found in the Appendix.[41] And the magistracy of the sect at Salerno issued a public notice, that

> the magistracy being informed that some superstitious fanatics, in order to discourage the Good Cousins, and to prevent the increase of their numbers, are circulating old bulls of excommunication and other follies, *inezie*, disgraceful to an enlightened age, declare that these things should be regarded with contempt; and especially as these bulls are the wicked fabrication of a party hostile to the country. It is, nevertheless, necessary to keep an eye upon

---

41   Appendix, No. V. The remonstrance is dated 20th September, 1820.

such fanatics; and towards them the vigilance
recommended in our 2d Article shall be directed. Salerno, 19th August, 1820.

The notions of the clergy are chargeable with
the same confusion and error as apply to the general arguments on political equality. But when the
foundation of an edifice gives way, all its angles appear distorted.

The secret societies at Naples had become a refuge for the timid during the fearful revolutions of
that city. The governments which had so quick-
ly succeeded each other inspired no confidence.
Hence the unprotected were glad to unite themselves closely, in hopes of some support in the vi-
cissitudes with which they were threatened. The
more enterprising rejoiced at finding themselves
exalted into judges on the great questions of the
nation; they imagined themselves the defenders
of the injured and oppressed. The secrecy and dis-
simulation required, cost nothing to the in habit-
ants of the south, among whom they have become
habitual. With them passive courage is highly
valued; and whosoever is not a traitor by nature,
seldom becomes so from fear of punishment or
torments. In the autumn of 1819, one Gaetano
Illuminati of Ferrara was arrested at Rome. The
proofs against him were so strong, that he attempted only a momentary denial of his attendance at
some illegal meetings, and was obliged to confess
that his letters, which had been intercepted by

the police, were sufficient to condemn him. Yet he peremptorily refused to name his accomplices, and declared that, to avoid useless importunities, he would starve himself to death. Accordingly, he persevered for twelve days in refusing to swallow the slightest nourishment, or to lie down to rest on his bed. The physicians of the prison, who visited him daily, perceived that he was dying; and he was at length only induced to renounce his purpose, by awakening his feelings of tenderness for his mistress and children, and by the promise of asking him no further questions as to his associates.

We must now return to the political history of the Carbonari during the reign of Murat. The suspicions of that sovereign were excited against them at an early period; and he began to hate and to persecute them. The anonymous author of a violent pamphlet against the minister Zurlo,[42] addressed to the Carbonari, ascribes the persecution to him. The following is his account of his proceedings; for the truth of which we cannot pledge ourselves: —

"No sooner," says the writer,

> was Zurlo created counsellor of state, than Joseph Bonaparte employed him to draw up a constitution, in which the *only article favourable to the nation, relates to the expulsion of foreigners from the offices of government.* This project Joseph never carried into effect. Afterwards, during a popular commotion, Murat

---

42 *Notizie sulla Condotta politica di Giuseppe Zurlo, terza edizione correttissima.*

H. R. H. Don Francis
Hereditary Prince of the Kingdom of the Two Sicilies and Prince of Calabria

attempted to conciliate the nation by ordering the election of representatives according to the singular method proposed in that constitution.

By Zurlo's management, a chief of division belonging to Saliceti's police was among the first members elected. The minister turned a deaf ear to the remonstrances of the provinces. He multiplied the officers of the Civil Administration, of the University, and of the Benevolent Institution. He lent his assistance towards the abolition of feudal rights, as he had done in 1799 towards the suppression of the 'Sedili' of Naples, only to increase the arbitrary power of the monarch.

The[43] offensive nature of these proceedings of government was perceived by many, and felt by all. The feeling of opposition it excited, gave rise to the associations of the Carbonari, whose object was to displace the ministers, and force a constitution from the government. The spirit of Murat and of his ministers was too well known by its despotic effects; it was therefore resolved to have recourse to the grand project of disorganising the army, in order to assist in recalling King Ferdinand, in the hope of obtaining a constitutional government from him; especially as much was expected at Naples, from the known virtues of the hereditary Prince; a confidence justified by the result.

Zurlo now perceived the danger of being exposed. He advised Murat to declare all the soldiers who were Carbonari infamous. The order of the day to that effect was read at head-quarters towards the end of 1813. But the societies increased notwithstanding. The universal de-

---

43   P. 14. of the same pamphlet.

sire for a constitution manifested itself even among the magistrates, and in the council of state. Serious disturbances took place in Calabria Citra. The Abruzzi followed the example on the report that the intermediate provinces had raised the standard of the constitution. At that moment Joachim was at Bologna: the only minister with him was Zurlo, minister of the interior, and of the southern Italian departments. It was he who issued the fatal decree of April 4th, 1814, in consequence of which so much blood was shed among the constitutionalists by the ambitious Nolli in the Abruzzi, and by the ferocious Manhès in the Calabrias.

The affairs of King Joachim began to decline after this period. Every one knows the event; but every one does not know that fear induced him to suspend those bloody executions, and to fill the prisons with Carbonari, in order to massacre them at leisure. They were indebted to the return of King Ferdinand for their deliverance. A very short time before the arrival of that monarch, who was recalled by the suffrages of the constitutionalists, the greater number of whom were Carbonari, Zurlo formed an absurd plan for diverting the public feeling, as follows:

In order to save the credit of the decrees against Carbonarism, and at the same time to change its object, Joachim was pleased to alter its form or name. Carbonarism was metamorphosed into agriculture; the Vendita became Pagliaja, straw hut, and the Good Cousins, Coloni, husbandmen. Murat created himself grand master of the order. Zurlo and his friends were the chief agents in this enterprize. Printed proclamations were circulated

by thousands in the provinces, but ineffectually: for an order, of which the sovereign was
grand master, his prime minister the second
in rank, and his agents of police the subaltern
officers, was immediately recognized as an association in favour of despotism, and not of the
constitution.

* * *

Meantime, while such were the measures adopted by Murat or his minister, the religious feeling
which had been diffused throughout the sect, the
agents of King Ferdinand who had introduced
themselves into it, and the arming of troops under some of the heads of the Order, who had set
up the standard of the good cause, gave rise to a
suspicion, that the Pope protected the Carbonari,
which a supposititious brief adroitly distributed in
manuscript confirmed.

Murat was so fully convinced of its truth, that
one of the first requests he made to Pius VII.,
when he met him at Bologna on his return from
France, 1814, was, that he would recall the Bull
issued in favour of the Carbonari. His Holiness
assured him, that he had not published the paper in question; and to the further request of
Joachim, that he would pronounce a public condemnation of the Carbonari, he replied, that the
Bulls of his predecessors were sufficient for the
purpose. However, he was no sooner arrived at
Rome, than an edict against the Free-masons and

secret societies appeared, signed by Cardinal Pacca, Pro-Secretary of State.[44]

To give an idea of the variety of opinions concerning the Carbonari, entertained not only in the
other countries of Europe, but in Naples itself, we
shall present the reader with some extracts from a
work on the subject published by Count Orloff, who
ascribes the origin of the sect to Queen Caroline of
Austria.[45] To these extracts, we will subjoin a few
explanatory notes, but it is impossible to reconcile
the different views of the opposite parties, one of
which considered the Carbonari, as Jacobins and
Republicans, and the other as the supporters of
the legitimate sovereignty of the Two Sicilies.

Extract I.—"In 1812," says the Count,

> the emissaries of Queen Caroline of Austria
> laid the foundations of an association, known
> by the name of Carbonari. This sect spread it-
> self rapidly through the Calabrias and Abruzzi,
> and thence throughout the kingdom, so that it
> is now beheved to consist of upwards of two
> hundred thousand members. The original ob-

---

44 For the Edict dated 15th August, 1814, see the Appendix No.

45 *Memolres sur le Royaume de Naples*—our first extract is from
Vol. II., p. 284.

A wretched pamphlet, entitled "*Breve idea della carboneria, sua origine nel regno di Napoli, suo scopo, sua persecuzione, e causa che fé nascere la setta de Calderari. Dal dottore
in legge Pasquale Tonelli—Napoli 1820, presso Pasq. Ti-
zano, Strada Cisterna dell'olio—No. 26*" repeats very nearly,
but without giving its authority, some of the assertions of the
Comte d'Orloff respecting the two sects.

ject of the association was to seize all opportunities of attacking and subverting the authority of Murat.

(Note.) —On examining the correspondence of Salvatore Bruni, in the first report of Saliceti, Minister of General Police, "on the conspiracy planned in the year 1807, against the French army in the kingdom of Naples, and against the person and states of H. M. Joseph Napoleon,"[46] the traces of a secret society are plainly discernible, and it is by that title, that Bruni designates his confederates. The emblems engraved on his passports and patents, the corresponding decorations, *viz.* heads and orange trees, which he earnestly recommends should be placed on the pedestals, on which the figures of the twelve quarters of Naples were to be exhibited, the incendiary proclamations in the name of Jupiter Thunderer,[47] are all so many marks of a secret association, as well as the letter[48] addressed by Queen Caroline, and dated Palermo, 10th May, 1807, to the society of Colonel Palmieri, Alia Societa del Colonello Palmieri. But all this is no proof that that secret society was that of the Carbonari.
Extract II.

The revolution which Lord William Bentinck had effected in Sicily, where the English were

---

46   Drawn up and printed in July, 1807.

47   Giove Fulminante--the name of one of the lodges of the Decisi.

48   Documents, No. IV. of the Reporf

possessed of the supreme authority, under the very eyes of the Court of Naples, having obliged the Queen to retire from public business, the Carbonari remained in a manner deserted, and without a rallying point. It was then that men of character and fortune perceived with terror, that these bands, composed in part of ferocious wretches already notorious by the excesses committed by them in 1799, menaced the public peace with the most cruel disasters, the effect of which it was not difficult to foresee. To avert these evils, and obtain such an influence as should enable them to direct the principles and movements of the society, they entered it themselves: nine of them, under the name of Capi di Vendite, were put at the head of the Vendite, or Baracche, names by which the various detached meetings of the order were designated. Thus organised, the society or sect united in its body men of all parties—Republicans, Constitutionalists, friends of Murat, and partisans of the Bourbons, and it is to the heterogeneous sentiments which then animated it, that its subsequent divisions are to be attributed.

In 1813, during the campaign of Saxony, Queen Caroline Murat, who was Regent in the absence of her husband, considered the Carbonari as a sect which could not be tolerated without compromising the stability of the then established government She therefore began the persecutions against them, which her husband followed up on his return to Naples after the battle of Leipzig, and it was probably this impolitic measure, which rendered his government so unpopular during the last year of his reign.

It was about this time, that the division of the sect took place. The number of the initiated had increased beyond calculation. Its leaders, aware of the difficulty of directing the movements of so great a multitude, conceived the plan of a reform, and executed it with secrecy and promptitude. The members who were retained, continued to bear the name of Carbonari, while those who were expelled took that of Calderari,[49] and an implacable hatred arose between the rival sects. Commotions followed, and the public tranquillity was often endangered by their disputes. Murat, alarmed, wavered for some time between the two parties, and at last determined on supporting the Carbonari who were most numerous. But it was too late. The intentions of the Congress at Vienna were known or suspected, and the people were unwilling to exert themselves in support of a man, whose fall seemed inevitable. Murat, despised by the Carbonari, and hated by the Calderari, perceived his throne totter, without a single effort of any party in his favour.

(Note.)—The assertion that men of character and fortune were placed at the head of the lodges, in order to oppose the ferocious bands of 1799, is not conformable with truth. Such persons have never been members. Neither did the Carbonari remain in inaction towards the period of Murat's fall, as the expression, "without a single effort of any party in his favour" seems to imply. But their efforts were hostile to Joachim, for they contrib-

49   Braziers—from Caldaro, a kettle.

uted to the dissolution of his army, and caused his precipitate retreat after the battle of Tolentino, by exciting disobedience and desertion. Whole battalions yielded to patriotic invitations so agreeable to their taste.

The society sent deputies into Sicily to offer the kingdom as a gratuitous gift to the Monarch. The Chevalier de' Medici treated with them. They demanded some concessions, which, as they asserted, had been promised to them, and a formal confirmation of their institution.

The sanction they pleaded for was refused, as well as the reduction of the taxes, and the establishment of constitutional privileges. They were simply told, that those to whom they applied were ignorant of the existence of such privileges: and it was recommended to them not to be too importunate.

Extract III.

> The Chevalier de' Medici, to whom, in the interim, the portfolio of Police was entrusted, seemed, on the King's restoration, to attach little importance to these internal divisions. Entirely occupied by the momentous care of the finances, he regarded both sects with indifference. The Carbonari attributed his inaction to fear, the Calderari augured from it, protection to themselves. The latter had witnessed the restoration with pleasure. It visited their wrongs on the head of their oppressor. The Carbonari, on the contrary, apprehensive of future persecutions which might give their rivals the advantage over them, took precautions for their safe-

ty. They drew the bonds of their union closer, and renewed their oaths of mutual and eternal assistance and defence.

Such was the state of the two sects at the moment when the Prince of Canosa became Minister of Police, in December, 1819. He adopted a different conduct from that of his predecessor with regard to the two mysterious associations. Persuaded that the Carbonari, who had been protected by Murat, during the last months of his reign, were irreconcilable enemies of King Ferdinand, he formed a plan of attack against them, whose success would have involved the subversion of the social order.

(Note.)—General Nunziante, the military commandant of the Calabrias, received a secret commission in 1816, to take information as to the number of sectaries in those provinces, in order to their suppression. He succeeded in corrupting one of the members; but a short time afterwards, the body of the informer was discovered, covered with wounds, and with a paper attached to it, addressed to the General, exhorting him to relinquish his enterprize, unless he wished to share the fate of the traitor. This man had been condemned to death in the presence of his own brother, who had no possible means of saving him, or warning him of his fate. It was on this occasion, that Nunziante sent information to Naples, that the means at his disposal were wholly inadequate to contend with the Carbonari, whose number in the Calabrias he estimated at fifty or sixty thousand.

Other instances of assassination of this kind have always been concealed, or at least they have been little noticed by the public; either because the Government has been afraid of exposing its weakness, while its agents trembled lest they should draw upon themselves the hatred of the sect; or because those who fell beneath the poignard were obscure or unknown individuals.

Extract IV.

> Canosa began his operations by drawing up a list of all the brigands, who had played a part in the sanguinary scenes of 1799, and embodied them in a new society, of which he himself became the chief, and to which he gave the name of Calderari del Contrapeso. He invited all the old Calderari to join his association, on account of their enmity to the Carbonari. He required the initiated to take an oath, whose principal articles were, passive obedience to his orders, and an engagement to exterminate, by every possible means, the Carbonari and the Freemason.

The following is the

Oath of the Calderari

"I. N. N. promise and swear upon the Trinity, as supreme director of the universe, upon this cross, and upon this steel,[50] the avenging instrument of

---

50 The Sikhs, a warlike nation of India, swear by the steel. A

the perjured—to live and die in the Roman Catholic and Apostolic faith, and to defend with my blood this religion, and the society of True Friendship, the *Calderari*, to which I am about to belong. I swear never to offend, in honour, life, or property, the children of True Friendship; I promise and swear to all the Knights, true friends, all possible succour that shall depend on me. I swear to initiate no person into the Society before I arrive at the 4th rank. I swear eternal hatred to all Masonry, and to its atrocious protectors; as well as to all Jansenists, Materialists,[51] Economists, and Illuminati. I swear, as I value my life—never to admit any of them into the Society of Friendship. Lastly, I swear, that if, through wickedness or levity, I suffer myself to he perjured, I submit to the loss of life as the punishment of my error, and then to be burnt: and may my ashes, scattered to the wind, serve as an example to the children of Friendship throughout the whole world. And so help me God, for the happiness of my soul, and the repose of my conscience."

(Note.)—The Minerva Napolitana[52] does not accuse the Prince of Canosa of the institution of the Calderari. A Bishop of the kingdom of Naples, says that work, whom it is unnecessary to name, formed a plan, or it was suggested to him at Rome, where he had taken refuge as hostile to the French

---

Highlander, to this day, considers no oath so binding as that by the point of his dirk or knife. —T.

51   Materialists, perhaps, should be read Molinists.

52   No. 7, p. 314.

government, of setting up a sect in opposition to the Carbonari, then erroneously looked upon as friendly to that government; on his return to Naples, and on being reinstated in his episcopal see, he assembled a number of persons of the middle and lower classes, and gave them the name of Calderari, or Braziers, in order to resist the Carbonari, as kettles resist coals, which are exhausted by burning under them!

Extract V.—

The new sect was divided into Curiæ. A central Curia in each province was directed to keep up a correspondence with all the others in its division. The minister took measures for ensuring a rapid and secret communication. He recommended to the chiefs to make proselytes, and distributed among them twenty thousand muskets, which he had procured from the Government arsenals, or purchased from private individuals.

This extraordinary scheme was drawing towards its execution, and had already spread terror throughout the provinces, when the King, having received information of what one of his ministers had dared to attempt without his knowledge, and having learned the true character of Canosa, deprived him of his office and banished him.

Thus terminated a plot which would have occasioned fresh miseries, and new scenes of blood; and which, although it produced no immediate result, has not been without consequences, alarming even at the moment in which we are writing, (1818).

In fact, the Carbonari, the sect opposed to the Calderari, have increased, and are still increasing in the kingdom. The two Societies are constantly and jealously watching each other; the slightest spark would suffice to produce an explosion, and amidst the havoc it would produce, some dexterous and daring votary of ambition would inevitably arise, to the eminent danger of the Government.

(Note.)—The Prince of Canosa left the ministry on the 27th June, 1816, after he had been in office about six months. A fanatical priest, whom he protected, namely the Padre Cotillo, had predicted that, on that day, venemous serpents would issue from the earth, and fire descend from Heaven, to exterminate the Neapolitans. The populace was terrified. The 27th of June was expected by the Lazzaroni with inexpressible anxiety. But the day proved perfectly fair; not a single cloud obscured the sun, and tranquillity was restored.

Three months after the exile of Canosa, the *Official Gazette* of the two Sicilies contained the following article: —

Since the publication of the Act by which His Majesty proscribed all Secret Societies, some individuals, the greater number of whom are of the lowest condition, and who had formerly displayed devotion to the King, and attachment to the Good Cause, have been in the habit of meeting in the secret conventicles, combriccole, of the Society called Calderari: His Majesty has directed them to be arrested and given up to justice.

Canosa retired into Tuscany. His confidant, the Abbate Latini, was banished to Ponza. This intriguing person, who had for some time been pensioned by England, was now accused not only of having betrayed the correspondence of Queen Caroline of Austria, whose private secretary he was, to Lord William Bentinck, but also of having forged several letters, which it was pretended she had written to Bonaparte and his agents. Latini died at Leghorn in 1819.

We have given above some traits of the character of Maghella, whom public opinion points out as the person who first gave influence to the Carbonari. And in addition to the anecdotes of Canosa, who has been always considered as the friend of the Calderari, contained in the extracts we have already made from Count Orloff's work, we shall present the same writer's more elaborate character of that minister.

It is worthy of remark, that both Maghella and Canosa were ministers of police; and that, having both obstinately followed their own private views, they but ill served the cause of their sovereigns.

Never has political police been so much employed as in the present age, and never was it before imagined so necessary to the preservation of thrones.

Never, on the other hand, has it proved so impotent in checking, or so dangerous in exciting, conspiracy and rebellion.

Extract VI.—Of Canosa, Count Orloff says:[53]

The Prince Canosa, called to the ministry of
the police, no sooner became possessed of a
power which may become as dangerous as it is
useful, conceived the fatal project of abandoning the system of moderation which had been
so prudently adopted. He granted to the lowest class of people the right of carrying arms,
which had before been severely prohibited. In
fact, he armed men, thirsting for blood, who
were always ready to enrich themselves with
the spoils of the more civilized. But he looked
upon the latter as enemies, because they professed sentiments different from his own. A
party man himself, he protected parties. Bands
of brigands organized themselves, and overran
the country in arms, giving out that they were
the agents of the minister of police, and under
his especial protection. The troubles produced
by the revolution, and the changes in the government, had established in the kingdom parties divided amongst themselves, and which,
notwithstanding the return of the legitimate
monarch, still subsist; and are preparing perhaps new sources of distress for this country, which for so many centuries has scarcely
ceased to be cruelly agitated.

The information Count Orloff's book had given
concerning the Carbonari, had been received with
avidity, and reappeared with more or less varia-
tion in the public journals, and more particularly

---

53   Memoires sur le Royaume de Naples, p. 283.

in *The Literary Gazette* of London. At length the Prince of Canosa took up the pen himself, to answer it in a work, entitled *I Piffari di Montagna, ossia Cenno estemporaneo di un Cittadino imparziale, sulla Congiura del Principe di Canosa, e sopra i Carbonari; Epistola critica diretta all'Estensore del Foglio Litterario di Londra, Dublino, nel Maggio,* 1820, pp. 118. The Mountain Pipes; or, an Extempore Essay, by an Lnpartial Citizen, on the Conspiracy of the Prince of Canosa, and of the Carbonari: a Critical Epistle addressed to the Editor of the London Literary Gazette: Dublin, May, 1820, pp. 118.

Although this publication is anonymous, the style and manner leave no doubt as to the author, in the minds of those acquainted with his former compositions.

He attempts to prove that he had neither the pecuniary means, nor the intention of distributing 20,000 muskets among the Calderari. Besides, the great numbers of the Carbonari, which existed at the very time he entered into office as head of the police, made him sufficiently conscious of the impossibility of destroying them by such expedients.

He defends himself against the accusations of cruelty and blood-thirstiness, by retracing his political life, during the whole course of which, he had never been sanguinary or vindictive. He ingenuously confesses the serious fault he had committed, while minister, in surrounding himself by subalterns, whom he himself denounces as stupid and corrupt; and excuses himself on account of the length of time during which he had been absent from his native country.

He refutes the assertion that the emissaries of Queen Caroline of Austria did, in the year 1813, found the Society of Carbonari, for the purpose of overturning the power of Murat; because, at the period in question, that princess was, in a manner, imprisoned in the country, without moneys without power, and narrowly watched by Lord William Bentinck.

He seems himself uncertain whether the sect be of French or of Italian origin; agreeing, however, with many persons at Naples, who assert that a French officer was the first who, in 1810, introduced its mysteries at Capua, the Society having been proscribed in his own country. It met at first with little encouragement, and for a long time the number of the initiated did not exceed seventy-five; but at length its real apostles appeared under the forms of the conscription, the *droits reunis*, and the free quartering of the military.

The Carbonari, kept under by an active system of police, only began to put their doctrines in practice when the French Empire had ceased to exist, and the power of Murat began to totter. They then imagined that the latter was intimidated, and on the point of yielding: but they were mistaken; for he instituted judicial proceedings against them, and caused some of them to be executed. At length (1815) the foundation of Joachim's throne being entirely sapped, and the Austrian army on the advance towards Naples, they chose that moment for revenge, and also to acquire a claim on the gratitude of King Ferdinand, by joining him, and by preventing a renewal of the popular massacres of 1799, which seemed to threaten the partizans of the French.

On this occasion, the Carbonari made a momentary junction with the Calderari, who were not enemies to monarchy in general, but only to the French usurpation. But the two factions neither had a common origin, nor did they ever profess the same principles. Many of the Calderari had, in fact, been associated with those who acted a part in the horrors of 1799; and the Prince of Canosa had nothing to do with those massacres. The name of Calderari, as he assures us, was first adopted in Palermo, not at Naples. In the former of these towns, there existed different companies of trades (*Maestranze*), which had enjoyed great privileges until they lost them by the constitution of Lord William Bentinck. The numerous company of Calderari (Braziers) felt the loss most keenly: they sent a deputation of their chief members to the Queen, to assure her that they were ready to rise and assert the injured rights of the crown. The flames of insurrection were communicated to the tanners, to the other companies, and to the majority of the people, and of the Neapolitan emigrants in Sicily.

Lord William Bentinck, aware of what was passing, put the Neapolitan emigrants on board ship, and sent them under a neutral flag to Naples, where Murat received them with a magnanimity scarcely to be expected from an enemy.

For this they were not grateful. They had hardly landed before they entered into the secret societies then conspiring against the French government; and their original name of Calderari was communicated by them to the conspirators, with whom they united themselves by new oaths at Naples.

An event which had recently happened in that city gave a sort of fashion to the epithet of Calderaro: this was the blowing up of the house of Saliceti by night, by one Domenico, a brazier by trade. The Prince of Canosa was suspected of being the instigator of this crime; and a strict search was commenced, in order to discover perpetrators. Several unfortunate wretches were executed on the strength of false evidence, forced out by torture, or procured by bribery. After their death an accident brought the real author and executor of the explosion to light. The whole was discovered through the simplicity of one of the private nuns,[54] named Theresa the Dyer, (Teresa la Tintora,) the aunt of the brazier. Even the model of the infernal machine was obtained: Domenico had escaped in time, and they could not arrest him in Sicily.

The name of Calderari of the Counterpoise (*Calderari del Contrapeso*), professing to be the creation of Canosa, is derived from a circumstance

---

54 Monaca di Casa: they wear the religious habit, and observe certain rules at home, without forming themselves into communities, and without being subject to monastic confinement.

which the author of the *Piffari di Montagna* reveals to us.

The existence of the Trinitarii (for so these sectaries entitled themselves before they were called Calderari) was better known to the Minister of Police, Canosa, than to his colleagues. He had been but a few days in office when there was a discussion in council on the secret societies which infested the provinces, even more than the capital. Two of the ministers addressed the Prince of Canosa seriously, and exhorted him to employ all his means against the Calderari, the atrocious remnant of 1799. The Minister of Police answered, that the real objects of all these secret societies were the same to enrich themselves at the expense of their neighbours, and to encroach upon the government, in order to usurp its power; that happily all these sects were at variance; that it was necessary to foment their mutual hatred as much as possible; that as the sect of Calderari was less strong and powerful than that of the Carbonari, it was politic to protect and favour the former, in order to counterbalance the latter, and to make use of them as agents and spies for the police against their rivals: and this was the more eligible, as the Trinitarii, or Calderari, took an oath to defend legitimate monarchy, while, on the contrary, the Carbonari took an oath to destroy it.

> In reasoning thus, the Prince of Canosa frequently employed the expression counterpoise, expecting that Calderarism would serve him as

a counterpoise to Carbonarism; and, notwithstanding the rule, that nothing said in council is
to be revealed, his speech transpired, and gave
rise to the reports concerning the institution, or
the reform, of the *Calderari del Contrapeso.*

These notices from the work of the Prince of Canosa possess a double interest, one derived from
their source, and the other from the consideration
that it is fair to attend to his justification after so
many accusations. It is, however, time to return to
the course of events at Naples.

In 1817 the Capitanata began to alarm the government, as well as the provinces of Lecce, Bari,
and Avellino: the inhabitants were possessed of a
number of small printing machines, and made use
of them to multiply manifestos, which they distributed in all directions. In these they demanded a
constitution from the King, and excited the people
to withhold the payment of the taxes in case of a
refusal. Three proclamations of this kind, various
in their expressions and tone, followed each other within a short period. The first was couched in
the language of entreaty. The second reminded the
King that "he had promised a constitution to his
people," and advised him to keep his royal word.
The third reproached him with delay. The people,
it said, have too long descended to entreaties, to
obtain what was due to the nation; and it intimated
that they would no longer pay the taxes unless they
obtained their constitution. The land-tax gather-
ers were threatened with death.

The ministry immediately despatched the Commissioner Intonti to Foggia, the chief town of the Capitanata. Intonti had been Attorney-General there, and was acquainted with several members of the different sects. He was entrusted with unlimited authority, and empowered to inflict summary justice, or rather injustice, by executing suspected persons, without trial. He preferred milder measures; and did not even signify to the authorities of the place the extent of his commission. On his arrival he summoned the most violent to his presence, and represented to them that it was impossible for the government to yield to their demands for a constitution, as neither the Emperor of Austria, whose troops were either still within the kingdom, or, at most, had only just passed the frontier, nor the other allied powers, would consent to such a measure.

Thus, for a time, tranquillity was preserved by persuasive measures; and the operations of the Carbonari were suspended. But the Capitanata was one of the foremost of the provinces in setting up the standard of the revolution. The first number of the *Amico della Constituzione,* drawn up by General Colletta, giving an account of the proceedings at Naples, from the 2d to the 6th of July, 1820, contains the following passage:

> The society of Carbonari was the focus of discontent, not because it propagated sentiments inimical to government, but because those whose opinions were hostile to government be-

came sectaries. Whoever therefore is curious
to trace the progress of public disaffection has
only to consult the progressive registers of Carbonarism. The number of Carbonari enrolled
during the month of March in the present year
amounted to 642,000.

Not satisfied with this multitude, the Carbonari
recruit daily throughout the kingdom, as well as
in Naples itself, where there are upwards of three
hundred and forty lodges. The Capri line of battle
ship alone contains three. They seek to make proselytes among the lower orders, particularly among
servants, and the Lazzaroni and fishermen, whom
they dread. Article 13th of the proceedings of the
Grand Diet of Salerno expresses openly the opinion of the meeting as to the importance of facilitat-
ing the reception of candidates, and of relaxing the
severity of the scrutiny.
Art. 13.

> Good Cousins, Dignitaries! The magistracy
> earnestly exhorts you to second the wish of the
> Grand Diet, expressed in Art. 78. Let us aug-
> ment our strength; let us be cautious how we
> exclude; let us again examine those who had
> been rejected in more suspicious times; let
> us exercise less rigour in admitting members.
> Let us refuse such only as are really unworthy
> and irreclaimable; those, for instance, guilty of
> defamation, qualified robbers,[55] and men with-

---

55 Perhaps the Assassini Pensionati—persons who, having been
    long in prison, are released with a pension, to take from them

out honour. Let us overlook corrigible faults; they will be corrected in our Baracche. Let us not reject those who have hitherto entertained opinions at variance with our own. They were then ignorant of the sanctity of our principles; if they be now alive to it, why refuse them the light? We pray you let us forswear all revenge, party-spirit, and faction. Let us endeavour, in short, to be a true people by uniting the whole nation with us, in order to be in a state to resist any foreign invasion whatsoever.

Art, 14.

Nevertheless, the magistracy, while it recommends indulgence in receiving members, proposes a certain means of assuring ourselves of those who enter our order. They must sign the oath; and this solemn act will be sent hither to be laid up in our archives. Such as cannot write must make the sign of the Cross in the presence of three witnesses, who must add their signature. This document will over-awe those who may wish to betray us.

This admonition not having produced all the effect desired, the magistracy adds, in the official journal of the republic:[56]

We are sorry to be obliged to express the most decided disapprobation as to the number of

---

the temptation of stealing. This is much practised at Rome, but with little good effect. T.

56   August 19, 1820. Art. 2

black balled candidates, (*anneramenti*,) announced by the last courier, there being no less than thirty in a single Vendita. Where will such a spirit of exclusion lead us, my Good Cousins? Supposing that 200 Vendite were to black-ball as many, not in a day or in a month, but in a year, we should not only lose six thousand faggots for our furnaces,[57] but we should create an army of 6000 enemies, without reckoning their friends and adherents. Our force would be but as one to a hundred; and, in the end, we should be reduced to a petty faction, unable to stand our ground against so many, who, in the event of a sinister result, not being of our body, would fall upon us. What absurd policy is this! What imprudence under circumstances not only not secure, but even dangerous! The magistracy therefore again earnestly recommends attention to the 13th Article of this Journal.

The legislative statutes of the Carbonari of the Western Lucanian Republic of 1818, section 5th, Art. 80, settle the following proportions between the population and the Vendite, whose effective members then consisted of the small landholders of the provinces, upon whom the land-tax weighed heaviest, and of the lower ranks of civil and military officers.

"In every district, Ordone, of any number of inhabitants not exceeding 1000, one Vendita may be established.

---

57 Faggots, *legni*, for the furnaces, *fornelli*—Carbonarc terms for members of their society

LUIGI MINICHINI
Illustre Primo Promotore della Libertà Nazionale

From 1,000 to 2,000—two.
From 2,000 to 4,000—three.
From 4,000 to 6,000—four.
From 6,000 to 8,000—five.
From 8,000 to 10,000—six.
From 10,000 to 1 8,000—eight."

In 1820 there were one hundred and eighty-two Vendite in Western Lucania, who sent deputies to the Grand Diet.

The persons who, from the beginning, have directed the labours of the Carbonari towards a political and constitutional object, have always been few in number. The impulse once given and received, they voluntarily withdrew behind the scenes, and have been forgotten. Even the late revolution brought but few to light.

The Canonico Menechini at Nola, and Lieutenant Morelli, only declared themselves because the exigency of the moment required it. Of these, Menechini alone seems to have been possessed of power. Sonnets in honour of the Canonico poured in on all sides; and copies of his portrait, engraved on stone, were sold by thousands in the streets of Naples.

He was appointed one of the members of the Committee of Public Safety: and during the first days of the revolution, his popularity enabled him twice to serve the cause of humanity. First, by calming the enraged populace assembled before the Royal Palace, at the time of the massacre of the Neapolitans, and of the sanguinary scenes at Palermo; and afterwards, by disarming the resentment of the ferocious Carbonari in the Field of Mars, when they threatened the lives of the ex-ministers Medici and Tommasi. But the reputation of Menechini soon declined, and he set out for Messina, to organize Carbonarism in Sicily. Some other individuals, all sons of St. Theobald, to use their own expression, have had the boldness to publish an account, authenticated by their signatures, of the contrivances and means employed by them at some distance of time, to bring about the revolution of July, 1820. They call it "An Historical Statement of the Facts which preceded and produced the Movement of the Sacred Battalion of Nola,"[58] for so they call that detachment of the cavalry, belonging to the Bourbon regiment, which deserted from Nola on the 1st of July, and was led by Silvati and Morelli to raise the standard of rebellion at Monteforte.

This pamphlet, which was speedily and cautiously withdrawn from circulation, is become exceedingly scarce, and we have therefore inserted it in the Appendix, as essential to the history of Carbonarism.

It is hardly necessary to observe, that an association of a million of men can no longer be considered as a secret society, although such a mass may be united by conventional signs unknown to others, as well as by oaths.

---

58 *Cenno storico sui Fatti die hanno preceduto e prodotto it Movimiento del Battagliotie Sacxo di Nola.*

The spirit of such an institution cannot fail to evaporate in a multitude which its chiefs can no longer controul. Besides, the object of overturning and destroying the government has been obtained: it is all that such a sect can bring about: it has not the power to create or to rebuild.

This inundating sea will retire of its own accord from the shores which it has laid waste; but it will leave the germs of other sects and associations, which, from their very essence, must be in opposition to existing governments.

It was long imagined that the Po was the boundary line of the sect in Italy; but this is a mistaken notion. Its principles are more widely diffused, but under different forms, and among various classes, which renders it less powerful than at Naples, where its members acted in concert, had absolutely the same interests, and looked upon events in the same light.

The Carbonari of the Roman States appear to be of higher rank, but of a more sanguinary and vindictive character. The account of their conspiracy, extracted from the minutes of the trial of the conspirators, is inserted in the Appendix to this work; from the time of its failure, they seem not to have attempted any important movements; but a number of individuals, especially in Romagna, have fallen singly beneath their daggers.

In the Lombard-Venetian kingdom, His Majesty the Emperor of Austria found it necessary to publish the following decree, dated August, 1820, against the Carbonari.

REGNO LOMBARDO VENETO

Notification

The society called Carbonari, which has spread it-self over various neighbouring states, has attempt-ed to make proselytes even in the Regal dominions of the Cæsars. From the investigations that have been made on the subject, the views of this Socie-ty have been discovered to be as dangerous to the state, as they are criminal in themselves, although they are not communicated by the superiors to every member of the society. By the express com-mand of His Majesty the Emperor and King, the object of these persons is publicly set forth, as a warning to each and every of his subjects.

THE PRECISE OBJECT THEN OF THE CARBONARI IS THE SUBVERSION AND DESTRUCTION OF ALL GOVERN-MENTS. It follows, therefore, that whosoever, being already acquainted with this object, has, notwith-standing, entered into the society of the Carbonari, is guilty of high treason, according to § 52 of the first division of our criminal code. And whosoever has not opposed the progress of the Society, or has neglected to inform against its members, agreea-bly to the §§ 54 and 55 of the same, has thereby become an accomplice, and has incurred the pen-alties provided by the law.

Therefore, from the date of the publication of this present Notification, no person can avail him-self of the excuse of not being aware of the precise object of the Carbonari; and consequently, whosoever shall enter into the said Society, or shall not oppose its progress, and inform against its members, shall be proceeded against according to the provisions of §§ 52, 53, 54, and 55, of the first part of the criminal code, set forth in the annexed extract from the statute.

Extract of Chap. 7. § 1. of the first division of the criminal code.

§ 52. He is guilty of the crime of high treason

(a) Who attempts any thing against the personal safety of the supreme head of the state:

(b) Who engages in any scheme tending to produce a violent revolution in the system of government, or to draw upon the state any danger from without, or to encrease an existing danger, whether such schemes be publicly or privately pursued, by persons singly, or associated by machination, by counsel, or by act; by force of arms or otherwise, by participation of secrets conducing to such an end, or by plots directed towards it; by instigation, by raising the people, by espionnage, or aid, by any action whatsoever, tending to such an object.

§ 53. This crime is punishable with death even if it fail, and is within the limit of a bare attempt.

§ 54. He who shall deliberately neglect to oppose a treasonable conspiracy, having it in his power without peril to himself so to do, becomes an accomplice in the crime, and is punishable with the severest imprisonment for life.

§ 55, He, also, who shall deliberately neglect

to give information before the magistrates, of persons known by him to be guilty of high treason, becomes an accomplice in the crime (unless it shall appear from the circumstances, that, notwithstanding such neglect, no evil consequence is to be apprehended.)—Such accomplice being punishable with severe imprisonment for life.

§ 56. He who shall have joined the secret societies alluded to, § 52. (b.) tending to high treason, but who shall afterwards repent, and give information to the magistrates concerning their members, regulations, objects, and enterprizes, while they are still secret, and their bad effects may be prevented, is assured that his full pardon will be granted, and his information kept secret.

* * *

It has been questioned whether the Neapolitan Carbonari aim at a republic, or whether they are satisfied with the constitution they have obtained.

The solution of this problem does not appear to be very difficult. Constitutional monarchies are so complicated, and their advantages are so little within the comprehension of ordinary minds, having hardly any direct influence on the inferior classes; they are unquestionably and necessarily so much more lavish in expenditure than absolute monarchies, that the mass of the people can only feel their just value, after a long and painful education, and after the lapse of many generations, harassed by political storms. Now it is the lower classes of society who compose the bulk of the Carbonari of Naples; and although the Spanish charter offers them numerous openings for democracy and licentiousness, it does not flatter their imaginations sufficiently to induce a sincere or lasting attachment.

The principal attractions of the present system consist in the popular courts, the voting by ballot, the power of trying and condemning by the list, even the most distinguished of their fellow citizens, and also of repressing such as might aim at rising above the ordinary level. These privileges also reconcile them to the continuance of their heavy taxes, and to that of the evils of the conscription, the motives or the pretexts of the revolution.

The high sounding words, independence, liberty, and equality, which are pepetually rung into the ears of the Carbonari; the whole system of education adopted by the order, its completely republican form, and even the very language of the sect, familiarize the people with the idea of a commonwealth, and keep it constantly in their view.

It would be very difficult to discover, in the maxims of Carbonarism, any thing that bears reference to a monarchy, even constitutional. That form of government would never satisfy the revolutionary fanatics and votaries of unreserved equality, for the general principle that every man is qualified to rise to any office in the state, tolerates with reluctance the exceptions of a king and royal family.

That the professors and pedagogues of the Carbonari do not dissemble on this head, their various publications furnish a convincing proof. The Catechisms, the Mentors, the Circulars, the Patents, and the Emblems of the sect, all speak a language not to be misunderstood. The following is a discourse pronounced by the orator of the Vendita of the Pythagoreans at Naples.

DISCOURSE[59]

Know, finally, that the object of respectable Carbonarism is to restore to the citizen that liberty and those right which Nature bestowed on us, and which tyranny itself, once, did not deny us. To attain to this object, it is necessary to try the virtue, and to consolidate the union of courageous and exemplary citizens: this is no trifling labour, since the cunning of political tyranny has interposed a thick veil between men's eyes and the sublime light of truth. Wretched mortals study those false maxims, which, leading to prejudice and superstition, envelope them in darkness, and induce them to lead a life of slavery and submission to ill treatment, blind to the origin of their misfortunes. Oh,

---

59 From a pamphlet entitled, *Istruizioni sul Secondo Grado di M. (maestro) Carbonaro redatto dal G. M, delia R. V. (Rispetabile Vendita) all' O. (ordone) Napoli. Pasquale Tavassi, sotto il titolo distintivo, I liberi Pitagorici.* Napoli, 1820, dai Torchi di Giuseppe Severino, Vico nuovo della pace. Nos. 18 and 19.

men! do you not hear the clank of the chains with which you are bound? They are fastened upon you by the tyrant.

By the law of Nature, he who seeks to destroy others should himself be annihilated. And are not kings, who, forgetting that they are men, proudly regard themselves as superior beings, and usurp the right of disposing of the blood of their fellow men, and of looking upon them as slaves, are they not the lords of the wives and children and possessions of those slaves? And yet honour, and homage and respect, are still paid to those infernal monsters![60] Oh, blindness of man!!!

But as the maxims of the Carbonari are founded on the simple principles of nature and reason, and on the doctrines of Jesus Christ, it belongs to them to overturn the throne raised by fanaticism and ambition, and to expel from it the monster who pollutes the whole creation. The blood of so many innocents, torn by main force from the bosoms of their families, and sent to perish in capricious wars; the blood of so many illustrious citizens slaughtered for speaking the language of truth; this blood, I say, calls on us for vengeance: and the number of our friends now groaning in fetters claim our assistance. Yes! the Carbonari, knowing what truth and justice are, and possessing humane and compassionate hearts, will one day vindicate the rights of man. Having found your conduct to be regular and zealous towards the Order, we have

---

60 Mostri Infernali.

admitted you into the chamber of honour, that is to say, among the sworn members of the Republic. You are come here to tender your lives for any service, when the Carbonari shall invite you to save your country from oppression.[61]

* * *

The oath administered to those admitted to the second rank in the same Vendita, *i. e.* the Pythagorean, breathes the same sentiments. "I swear eternal hatred against all tyrants, and their satellites, and to avail myself of all opportunities to destroy them." Another remarkable proof of the prevalence of the same sentiments is the prayer of a G. C. Apprentice, affixed to the Mentor.[62]

---

61 After the discourse, the symbols were explained as in the other Vendite, but with some difference, probably such as to suit the various degrees of information possessed by the members. The instructions contained in the master s catechism suggests, that, of the earth may be said—"The earth reminds us that we should not be ambitious or covetous of greatness, for we must all be changed to dust. Life is no other than a short journey, *breve passo.* Of the thorns the orator may say,—"The crown of thorns shows us, that under despotism, instead of tasting of the sweet and precious productions of the earth, and the delights of liberty, we gather bitter thorns, which are for ever tormenting us, and therefore we should seek to free ourselves once for all from the yoke of tyranny."

62 *Il Mentore di un B. C. App.*

A. G. D. G. M. D. U.
(*Al Gran Dio Gran*
Maestro del Universo)

Carbones succensi sunt ab eo.—Ps. xvii.[63]

O Thou Great God, Author and Master of Nature, Thou who hast formed men to be free and independent, and not to be the tyrants and oppressors of their brethren. Thou who kindlest in the hearts of thy children the holy flame of charity, of that charity which considers all men upon the earth as forming one family! Thou who guidest through the desert of life those souls which are faithful unto Thee, and protectest them by thy omnipotence; who smitest with the axe of thy vengeance the thrones that are raised upon profane principles, and erectest upon their ruins the rightful sovereignty of the people: receive the homage of adoration and respect which we render up to Thee from the bottom of our hearts. Protect the people of the free Carbonari, who humbly invoke Thee: and if Thou hast defended them from the injuries of arbitrary power and ferocious tyranny; if Thou hast made them feel the gift of thy all-powerful patronage, continue to stretch over them thy beneficent hand. Permit them not to degenerate from the divine law. May virtue every where accompany them. May they be enabled to defend those principles which they have sworn to maintain, even with

---

63   In the English version, Ps. xvii. v. 8.—T

their blood, and may they continue in unanimity and concord until the sun

Shall shine upon human miseries.[64]

Thanksgiving, honour, and glory to Thee for ever.

* * *

Such readers as may be inclined to interpret these expressions in a less sinister sense, may read the last stanza of the lyrical motto which decorates the title-page of the Constitution of the Eastern Lucanian Republic, printed at Potenza, its headquarters, 1820.

> Ma tua pianta radice non pone
> Che su' pezzi d' infrante corone:
> Ne si pasce di fresche ruggiade.
> Ma di sangue di membra di Rè[65]
>
> MONTI.

It cannot be said that the chiefs of the Eastern Lucanian Society are men without authority or in-

---

64   "Risplenderà sulle sciagure umane."

65   Thy plant will strike its roots alone
    'Midst fragments of a shatter' d throne;
    Nor freshest dews its leaves may nourish,
    'Tis regal blood must make it flourish.

    The ode to Liberty, consisting of only two stanzas, of which the one quoted is the second, is not printed in the ordinary editions of Monti's works. —T.

fluence, because the principal members of its supreme magistracy have been elected deputies to the National Parliament. All the republics of the Carbonari do not, however, so shamelessly preach the disgusting doctrines of horror and Jacobinism.

The Elder Sister, *i. e.* the Western Lucanian Republic, is more crafty in the pursuit of its object, and conceals it better. It sometimes assumes the credit of wishing to support the constitution, and will surely not fly in the face of the monarchy till the danger of foreign invasion shall be past.

In the detail of the fundamental principles of its Statute of organization, it explains its intentions more mildly.

The Representatives of the Western Lucanian
Republic, met in Grand Diet:[66]

Wishing to consecrate anew the social ties of the Carbonari of Western Lucania, formed by the statute of the year 1, according to the reiterated manifestations of the general feeling, and to the declaration of the first principles which were its basis, and which must secure its duration for the common welfare—By virtue of the authority received from the people, and in their name, have sanctioned and do sanction, &c.

---

66   *Nuovo Statute organico della Carboneria della Republica Lu-
cana Occidentale, (Principato citra) Sanzionato nella Gran
Dieta deir anno 2, (1818.) Ordone centrale di Salerno.* Dalla
Tipografia della Rep. Luc Occid. (Printed August, 1820.)

CHAP. I.

Of the Creation of the Order;
of its Object and its Essential Relations

Art. 1. One single united society shall be formed of the Carbonari of Western Lucania.

Art. 2. The boundaries of its territories shall be those of the pagan province of Principato Citra.

Art. 3. The Western Lucanian Republic shall be one, indivisible, and independent.

Art. 4. The Carbonari of the W. Lucanian Republic shall preserve inviolate the ties which unite them by confederation with all the Carbonari dispersed over the face of the earth.

Art. 5. The Carbonari of the W. Lucanian Republic will naturally be the friends and allies of all associations of liberal and philanthropic men.

Art. 6. This Society shall propose for its object the general wish of the Order, which particularly aims at the diffusion of knowledge, the uniting of the different classes of citizens in the bonds of love, the impressing of a national character on the people, in order to interest them in support of their country and religion: the destruction of the source of crimes by the inculcation of good morals: the protection of the feeble, and the relief of the unfortunate.

CHAP. III.

Of the Form of Goviernment of the Western Lucanian Republic

"The Republic shall be governed, first, by a Senate to propose laws and to debate; 2dly, by a representation of the people to decide; and 3dly, by a magistracy to execute."

On the first revolutionary movement at Naples all these republics of the Carbonari emerged from their obscurity, and seized the command of the Government, till the King had signed the decree adopting the Constitution of the Spanish Cortes. The Eastern Lucanian Republic was so conspicuous by its vehemence, that not only foreigners, but even the inhabitants of Naples, and those members of Government initiated into the Order, thought that it intended to detach itself altogether from the body of the kingdom, and to form a sort of insulated state in its very centre.

This report continued in circulation, even for some days after the Spanish Constitution had been proclaimed, and sworn to at Potenza, and the magistracy found it expedient to publish the following Advertisement:

From the Patriotic Journal of Eastern Lucania, Potenza, 20th July, 1820[67]

Advertisement

Some evil disposed persons have raised an outcry, because the Government of the Carbonari of this district has styled itself the Eastern Lucanian Republic. They have represented this as an approach to a democratic constitution, and have thereby endeavoured to agitate the public mind. *Without thinking it worth while to advert to the Constitution of Carbonarism, which should be concealed from the profane,* we beg leave to inform these oligarchical pedants, that the term Republic is not confined in its application to a state in which either the *many* or the *few* govern, but it signifies also, any government lawfully constituted, as Rousseau teaches in his *Social Contract*, B. ii. chap. vi. where he thus expresses himself—"I call every state, governed by the laws, under every possible form of administration, a Republic: provided that public interest alone governs, and where the public wel-

---

67 The Lieutenant-General F. Pignatelli Strongoli, sent about this time to Basilicata and Potenza, quieted some tumults and dissensions which had agitated that province during fifty days. Libels and incendiary letters were distributed, the public authorities were disregarded, the public money was retained. The most violent talked of marching against the capital, and the election of the new magistrates of the Carbonari took place in the midst of the greatest confusion, and the threats and the poignards of the rioters.

fare is considered, every legitimate government is a Republic."

* * *

The Declaration "In the name of God," of the 6th July, and the "Notice" published on the 8th of the same month, are documents that appear to us sufficiently curious to be inserted in this place. Among other interesting matter, the restrictions to be imposed on the executive power, and the imperfect state of the constitution, which is assumed, are not the least deserving of attention.

DECLARATION IN THE NAME OF GOD, AND UNDER THE AUSPIRCES OF THE NEAPOLITAN PEOPLE

Art. 1. The united citizens aim at rendering the monarchy constitutional, for upon that must depend the welfare and prosperity of the nation, which has been condemned for so many centuries to slavery and degradation.

Art. 2. The national assembly which is about to be confirmed will endeavour to obtain every possible diminution of the taxes. And to give an immediate proof of the interest it takes in the condition of the indigent class of citizens, as well as in that of the proprietors, it assumes to itself at once the power of decreeing the diminution of one half of the duty on salt, one third of the land tax, and the abolition of the conscription.

Art. 3. No tumult or crime should obscure the fortunate epoch of the regeneration of the country. Whoever therefore dares to interrupt the public tranquillity, or attempt the honour, the liberty or the property of the citizens, or in any way whatever offend religion or its ministers, shall be tried and severely punished by a military commission.

Art. 4. That social order may effectually be preserved, the laws actually in force shall continue to be observed till the publication of the new legislative code.

Art. 5. All the magistrates and officers of government, in whatsoever branch of administration, shall remain in their situations, provided that, within twenty-four hours from the publication of the present Declaration, they take the oath of fidelity to King Ferdinand I., and to the Constitution, to be administered to them by the highest ecclesiastical dignitary in the town where they reside, and at a public ceremony to take place in the principal church:—the constitution is established on the following basis:

1. The King is to have the executive power only.

2. He cannot make or interpret the laws, *pardon, confer appointments, impose contributions, or make peace or war.* These rights belong to the people, which is to be represented by its legitimate deputies.

3. At the end of every year the Ministers of government shall give a public account of their transactions.

4. The citizens are to enjoy full liberty of thought and of the press.

5. Situations are only to be bestowed on those born and residing in the kingdom.

6. The preservation of public order should be the care of every citizen; but this charge is entrusted (under responsibility) especially to the officers of the militia, to the Ecclesiastics, to the Syndics, Decurions and principal proprietors.

7. In order that the party-spirit which divides the nation may cease, and that all the citizens may form a people of brothers, it is forbidden to insult or offend in any way whatever, those who have hitherto entertained an opinion contrary to liberal ideas, and who, *convinced of their error* shall have the right of again taking their place among honest citizens.

The country receives them with transports of joy.

8. On the other hand, whosoever seeks to check or oppose the operations of the Constitutionalists, either by word or deed, shall be tried and punished by a military commission—attempts to discourage and alarm constitute the former of these offences.

9. The national debt is guaranteed.

10. All military ranks and honours, with their corresponding pensions of whatever nature, and for whatever service they may have been granted, are confirmed.

11. All such soldiers and citizens, as distinguish themselves in the service of the good cause, have a sacred claim on the national gratitude. The coun-

try will generously reward their labours. And those soldiers who are the first to support the operations of the constitutionalists shall immediately be promoted a step.

12. The Ministers of religion are invited to offer up public prayers to Almighty God, that he may protect the Neapolitan nation in its glorious enterprize.

13. The present declaration shall be published by the Syndics and Rectors upon the altar, and read at the head of the companies, who compose the constitutional army.

(Signed.) The orator of the Senate of the Eastern Lucanian Republic certifies that this Declaration is conformable to the original.

EGIDIO MARCO GIUSEPPE.
Potenza, 6th July, 1820.

Extract from the Patriotic Journal
of Eastern Lucania

"Advertisement, (8th July, 1820)"[68]

The Senate of the Eastern Lucanian Republic represents the people of Basilicata, and supports their rights at the price of its own blood.

Until the constitution of Ferdinand I. shall be published, and accepted by the deputies of the people of all the provinces of the kingdom, no act or decree of the late government shall, from this day forward, be published or observed in the territory of Eastern Lucania or Basilicata.

The administrative and judicial authorities shall exercise their functions in the name of the Constitution and of the King; and the articles contained in the Declaration printed at Potenza the 6th July, 1820, which has been proclaimed to the people of Basilicata, shall be entirely observed, till the said Constitution be given.

Whoever opposes this, is declared an enemy to his country and the interests of the people.

---

68 The Lieutenant-General F. Pignatelli Strongoli, sent about this time to Basilicata and Potenza, quieted some tumults and dissensions which had agitated that province during fifty days. Libels and incendiary letters were distributed, the pubhc authorities were disregarded, the public money was retained. The most violent talked of marching against the capital, and the election of the new magistrates of the Carbonari took place in the midst of the greatest confusion, and the threats and the poignards of the rioters.

The command of the constitutional forces of Eastern Lucania is entrusted to General Sponsa and Colonel Corbo, who, having particularly distinguished themselves in the defence of our cause, have merited the gratitude of the country, according to the 11th article of the said Declaration.

The President, CARLO CORBO.
First Assistant, GAETANO SCALEA.
Second Assistant, GERMANO MARONE.
Secretary, GIUSEPPE SICORELLA.
GAETANO CORRADO.

Senators
MARCO LACAPRA.
LUIGI SPERA.
BONAVENTURA MARONE.
PASQUALE MANTA.
GEN. BAGNULO.
PASQUALE CILENTO.
FR. MARONE, G. M. dei Pitiliani.

It has been observed, that the Carbonari are in great measure independent on the judicial authorities. This is still more the case with regard to the executive and legislative powers, which they look upon with suspicion. Hence their anxiety to form leagues, and provincial republics, in order to keep a watchful eye even upon the Supreme Vendita at Naples, which they consider too close to the government. The project for the confederacy, communicated by the Supreme Magistracy of Salerno to the General Assembly of the Carbonari, places the fears and the wishes of the order in the clearest light.

The reader must not suffer himself to be deceived by some expressions of respect towards the royal family, and of attachment to the new constitution in this singular document: for the King, the Hereditary Prince, the Ministers and their agents, the army and its officers, all in short, who possess power or influence in the state, are not the less exposed to continual accusations of bad faith, and of secret intentions hostile to the sect and to the revolution. Such members of the Parliament, also, as are not returned from the body of the Society itself, or such as lean towards the Ministry, or even towards moderate measures, are obnoxious to such attacks.

The consciousness of having been the principal movers of the rebellion, and of having raised the political storm which impends over the country, induces the Carbonari to gain as many accomplices as possible, openly to implicate such as are backward in acknowledging their fellowship, and to exact security from all new members. Hence proceed their memorials, and addresses, and the violent measures forced upon the government.

Hence, also, their anxiety never to lose sight of its operations, and, if possible, to controul and direct them.

* * *

Journal of the Western Lucanian Republic.
No. 2.

From the Central District of Salerno, the 19th of the nth month, year 3. (19th of August, 1820.)

PROJECT OF CONFEDERATION

Respectable Good Cousins,
The Magistracy exercising the Supreme Executive power of the Western Lucanian Republic, taking into serious consideration that, although the moral and physical efforts of the Carbonari, generously seconded as they are by our august monarch Ferdinand, and his destined successor to the throne. Prince Francis, Vicar General of the kingdom, have attained their object of overturning a despotic government. Much still remains to be done, in order that the constitutional government may be consolidated and preserved from iniquitous plots within, and from aggression from without.

Maturely considering that, although the Carbonari are already united by feelings, principles, and force of action; yet it is necessary that such a confederacy should be bound together by a solemn act, in order that, with combined and well-directed forces, they may be enabled to resist any hostile attack whatever, and to sustain the Bourbon dynasty on the constitutional throne.

To obtain this salutary result, it proposes the following articles.

I. There shall be a confederacy between the Carbonari of those provinces, not excepting the province of Naples, which are already formed into regular governments. Every one of them, however, shall preserve its own independence, with sovereign, legislative, and executive power, within the limits of its own territory.

II. The confederacy may be afterwards extended to the Carbonari of other provinces, adopting as a principle, that the territory of every Republic shall be circumscribed in the same manner as the Pagan provinces. But they must first establish a regular government, summoning, as occasion shall require, one or more deputies from every Vendita to the General Diet, in order to establish its own internal independent organization, and the election of its own magistrates.

III. Meanwhile, till such regular government be established in the provinces that are not yet organized, insulated Vendite, and even tribes, may attach themselves to the neighbouring governments; being obliged, however, to send deputies to the general diet of their own province, and afterwards to return to the government of the same, as soon as it shall be reduced to form.

IV. The object of the confederacy will be,

    1. The consolidation and preservation of the constitutional government of the monarchy.

2. The defence of our most holy religion, as well as of the august reigning Bourbon dynasty.

3. Our mutual defence against the blind enemies of the Order of the Carbonari.

4. The direction of the public spirit to the principles of sound and correct morality, by means of education and instruction, in order that religion and the legitimacy of thrones may be respected.

5. The active and efficacious co-operation of all our moral and physical efforts to obtain such important objects.

V. The confederacy should be governed,

1. By a periodical congress, composed of three representatives from every Republic.

2. By a permanent deputation composed of one third of the said representatives, one of each region, to be chosen from the body of the congress itself

VI. The permanent deutation shall always act on behalf, and in the name of the congress. The duties of the same shall be as follows:

1. To examine and pronounce sentence upon the acts of government; to watch over the conduct of its agents; to effect the reform of abuses by moral influence, and by petitions, if necessary.

2. To suggest to the Confederate Republics, all means and measures which can conduce to the national prosperity, and to ac-

quaint them, on the other hand, with their wants.

3. To open treaties with philanthropic and liberal societies in other countries, and to interest them in the general welfare of humanity.

4. To form into independent Republics, all the provinces not yet organized, and to admit them to the confederacy.

5. To give the private watch-word every half year to all the Confederate Republics.

6. To keep an eye upon every attempt which may be made against the welfare of the nation, from within and from without.

7. If the country or royal family are in danger, or if any attempt be made to overturn the constitution, to declare it upon sufficient evidence to the Confederate Republics; to wait the deliberations of the same, and then to act according to the instructions which shall be communicated.

8. To call an extraordinary meeting of the congress, when necessary.

9. To put in motion the whole or a part of the forces of the Carbonari, and to appoint a temporary commander-in-chief, even without the consent of the Republics, or of the congress; but only in the following most urgent cases that do not admit of delay.

   1. An attempt against the royal family.
   2. An anti-constitutional revolution.

   3. An unforeseen hostile attack from without, by land or by sea; in which cases the deputation shall be most strictly and personally responsible.

VII. The duties again of the congress shall be:

1. To fix the place of its own sittings, as well as that of the permanent deputation, with the power of varying it according to circumstances; preferring the most central provinces, such as the two principal, Terra di Lavoro and Naples.

2. To fix the regulations for the internal management as well of the congress as of the deputation.

3. To fix the probable expenditure of the Confederacy.

4. To fix the contingent of the forces of every Republic.

5. To examine all the operations of the permanent deputation, to approve or censure them, especially if the forces of the order be in motion.

6. To propose to the Confederate Republics, three illustrious personages, so as to be able to select from them a commander-in-chief of the forces of the Carbonari by a plurality of votes.

7. To accommodate with prudence and wisdom, the disputes which may arise among the Republics.

8. To preserve uniformity in the journals of

proceedings, and in the catechisms of the order.

9. To propose to the Confederate Republics, the improvements of which the respective statutes may be susceptible.

VIII. Neither the congress nor the deputation should ever oppose the deliberations of the parliament, or the acts of government, by active measures, but merely watch over them to inform the Republics and await their determination.

They can neither impose any contributions nor dispense aid. Much less can they initiate proselytes, grant rank, honours, distinctions, or punish any one, on pain of being prosecuted as guilty of high treason against the people.

IX. Besides the extraordinary convocations, the congress will meet regularly on the 18th of September of every year. The duration of its deliberations shall not be less than fifteen days, nor shall it exceed a month. The place of meeting shall for this year be at Salerno, several Republics having expressed a wish to this effect.

X. The duration of the congress shall be three years. Every year, however, one third of the members shall vacate their seats by lot, and be replaced. The deputation shall be renewed every year. At the end of the three years, it will be determined whether the Confederacy shall continue, be modified, or dissolved; and this determination will depend on observing whether the constitutional government be completely established.

XI. No member of the deputation, even if he have a legitimate motive, shall quit his post without acquainting the body, and the Republic he represents, on pain of having his name burnt, besides being burnt in effigy, if he acts so from prevarication or treachery.

XII. The Republics which shall find this project adapted to the general good are requested to send their act of adherence as soon as possible to the magistracy exercising the supreme executive power of the Western Lucania (Salerno), directing their letters in the Pagan style, to D. Pietro Sessa, the secretary of the said magistracy. If they have any observations to make on the less essential parts of the project, they may reserve them for the discussion of the congress, which, for the first time, shall be considered as an assembly representing the Confederate Republics of the Carbonari.

Fortunately, this sect, which arrogates to itself so much independence, and the right of interference in all public affairs, is daily losing ground by its own imprudence. It is a Jacobine or radical party, such as is to be found elsewhere, far beyond the limits of the two Sicilies. The curiosity of its members is no longer irritated by an unknown object. Their zeal is no longer kept alive by mystery. The ceremonies and emblems have lost their power as symbolical of great events, and a happy futurity; for habit has rendered them familiar and uninteresting. The abuse of them has often made them ridiculous,[69] and the lower orders of candidates have learned to speculate more on the alms which they expect in case of want, from the Society, than on the marvellous secrets to be revealed to them.

The old members have begun to look down with contempt on the new, although they are themselves disappointed and disgusted with a reality by no means corresponding with the expectations they had formed.

Free-masonry appears now to be destined as a retreat for such Carbonari as begin to despise their old associates, and who are glad of a pretext for joining a more respectable order. The lodges of the Free-masons are daily increasing in number at Naples, and its publications are read with much more avidity than those of the Carbonari. It is not uncommon to hear the expression, "Such an one is more than a Carbonaro, he is a Free-mason."

The government follows the example of the Spanish Cortes, and seems inclined to put in force the decree of Madrid against clubs and political so-

---

69   The fair sex has thought fit to form societies, and as Free-Masonry had its lodges of "Mopses," so Carbonarism tolerated female lodges, under the name of *Vendite delle Giardiniere*: i. e. Lodges of Garden-women. These ladies boast of their Good Cousinship, and the glorious title of *Giardiniere* figures in their publications, especially in their patriotic verses; which will not however, we think, turn the heads of the Neapolitan youth. Several of them, now before us, are the productions of the muse of the Cousin Giardiniera G. A. D. R. and are addressed "To the Glorious Young Men of the Country"—*La C. Giardiniera G. A. D. R. ai Gloriosi Giovani della Patria.*

cieties, as the best means of attacking the sect.

Some general officers, particularly General Florestan Pepe, have shown that they are not afraid of the Vendite in their corps, who endeavoured to influence their fellow-soldiers: and General Carrascosa shows them so little deference, that when certain officers, who had been disgraced for cowardice in 1815, demanded re-admittance into the service, alleging, among other reasons, their attachment to Carbonarism, he answered, "*Poco mi premeva di S, Teobaldo, e del Grand' Architetto del Universo.*" What care I for St. Theobald, &c.

Thus the natural progress of the evil itself has been the means of discovering the remedy. It is this remedy, which the small number of the friends of order look to as the only port of safety; and good policy will be extremely cautious not to shut that opening against them, by having recourse to violence and persecution.

* * *

As a supplement[70] to the account we have given of the Secret Societies, particularly the Carbonari, it may not be uninteresting to retrace some of the

---

70 To the Reader. A sheet of the M.S. of his work was unfortunately lost. It contained the introductory part of this Supplement, as far as the words celebrated mass before he began the conference. As both the Author and Translator are on the Continent, the Editor could only supply the following paragraphs from memory; they contain, however, the only facts stated in the original.

events connected with General Church's campaign, as it has been called, against the brigands of Calabria and the Abruzzi. The tranquillity of those provinces had been disturbed by bands of outlaws, who, under the names of the different Secret Societies, Carbonari, Decisi, Filantropi, &c. and even sometimes without any such pretence, way-laid travellers, interrupted the course of public justice, and went so far as to seize the government supplies. One of the most celebrated leaders of those gangs was the Priest Ciro Annichiarico. Driven from society by his crimes, he had taken refuge in the mountain forests, and having collected a desperate band of outlaws like himself, he had long carried on his depredations unmolested.

Upon the adoption, however, of vigorous measures by the government, in order to put down the brigands, he took the alarm, and determined, if possible, to persuade all the various bands of outlaws and brigands of whatever faction or denomination, to make a common cause, and to oppose the march of the King's troops, with all the forces they could muster. He imagined that the more formidable they could make themselves, the better terms they might expect when they came to treat, and he was the more eager to induce the chiefs of the bandits to join him, as he had less hope of personal indulgence, being already under sentence of at least perpetual imprisonment for murder. The Vardarelli, it was believed, who had made themselves very conspicuous by their activity in plundering both private individuals and the public, had obtained good terms, yet they would not have objected, perhaps, to rebel anew, if they could have hoped to better those terms. Ciro, therefore, invited them, and the heads of other bands, to a personal conference, in order to treat of the measures to be pursued against General Church, and they accordingly had two different interviews, the first at the end of 1816, or the very beginning of 1817, in a little deserted chapel, where he celebrated mass before he began the conference, and the second in the month of March or April, 1817, in a farm between S. Eramo and Gioja. Gaetano Vardarelli differed as to the propriety of a junction:

> He represented that it was better to act in concert, but separately, and to avoid a general insurrection, of which they might easily become the victims. As long as our bands are not numerous, government will be deceived, and make war upon us feebly, as it does now; but as soon as we form ourselves into a more important body, it will be forced to send more troops against us.

Vardarelli at this moment had already obtained a capitulation, and was in the service of King Ferdinand; but he would have been ready to quit it, if the enterprize of Ciro had been attended with marked success: he therefore kept himself in readiness, and remained at hand to wait the event.

Ciro Annichiarico, born of parents in easy circumstances, in the little town of Grottaglie, was destined to the ecclesiastical profession, and entered it very young. His brothers are respectable farmers; his uncle, the Canonico Patitaro, is a man of learning and information, and never took any part in the crimes of his nephew. The latter began his infamous career by killing a young man of the Motolesi family in a fit of jealousy. His insatiable hatred pursued every member of the family, and he exterminated them one after the other, with the exception of a single individual, who succeeded in evading his search, and who lived shut up in his house for several years, without ever daring to go out. This unfortunate being thought that a snare was laid for him when people came to tell him of the imprisonment, and shortly after of the death of his enemy; and it was with difficulty that he was induced to quit his retreat. Ciro, condemned for the murder of the Motolesi, to fifteen years of chains, or exile, by the tribunal of Lecce, remained there in prison four years, at the end of which time he succeeded in escaping. It was then that he began, and afterwards continued for several years, to lead a vagabond life, which was stained with the most atrocious crimes. At Martano, he penetrated with his satellites into one of the first houses of the place, and after having offered violence to its mistress, he massacred her with all her people, and carried off 96,000 ducats.

He was in correspondence with all the hired brigands; and whoever wished to get rid of an enemy had only to address himself to Ciro. On being asked by Captain Montori, reporter of the military commission which condemned him, how many persons he had killed with his own hand, he carelessly answered, *"E chi lo sa? saranno tra sessanta e settanta."* Who can remember? they will be between sixty and seventy. One of his companions, Occhiolupo, confessed to seventeen; the two brothers Francesco and Vito Serio, to twenty-three: so that these four ruffians alone had assassinated upwards of a hundred!

The activity of Ciro was as astonishing as his artifice and intrepidity. He handled the musket and managed the horse to perfection; and as he was always extremely well-mounted, found concealment and support, either through fear or inclination, every where. He succeeded in escaping from the hands of the soldiers, by forced marches of thirty and forty miles, even when confidential spies had discovered his place of concealment but a few hours before. The singular good fortune of being able to extricate himself from the most imminent dangers, acquired for him the reputation of a necromancer, upon whom ordinary means of attack had no power among the people, and he neglected nothing which could confirm this idea, and increase the sort of spell it produced upon the peasants. They dared not execrate, or even blame him in his absence, so firmly were they persuaded that his demons would immediately inform him of it. On the other hand, again, he affected a libertine character; some very free French songs were found in his portfolio when he was arrested. Although a priest himself, and exercising the functions of one when he thought it expedient, he often declared his colleagues to be impostors without any faith. He published a paper against the Missionaries, who, according to him, disseminated illiberal opinions among the people, and forbade them on pain of death to preach in the villages, "because, instead of the true principles of the Gospel, they taught nothing but fables and impostures." This paper is headed, "*In nome delta Grande Assemblea Nazionale dell'Ex-Regno di Napoli, o piuttosto dell'Europa intera, pace e salute,*" "In the name of the Great National Assembly of the Ex-Kingdom of Naples, or rather of all Europe, peace and health."

He amused himself sometimes with whims, to which he tried to give an air of generosity. General d'Octavio, a Corsican in the service of Murat, pursued him for a long time with a thousand men. One day, Ciro, armed at all points, surprised him walking in a garden. He discovered himself, remarking that the life of the General was in his hands, "but," said he, "I will pardon you this time, although I shall no longer be so indulgent, if you continue to hunt me about with such fury." So saying, he leaped over the garden wall and disappeared.

Having hidden himself, with several of his people, behind a ruined wall at the entrance gate of Grottaglie, the day when General Church and the Duke of San Cesario, accompanied by some horsemen, reconnoitred the place, he did not fire upon them; he wished to make a merit of this before the military commission, but it was probably the fear of not being able to escape from the troops who followed the general, that made him circumspect on this occasion.

Ciro's physiognomy had nothing repulsive about it; it was rather agreeable. He had a verbose, but persuasive eloquence, and was fond of inflated phrases.[71] Extremely addicted to women, he had mistresses, at the period of his power, in all the towns of the province over which he was constantly ranging. He was of middle stature, well made, and very strong.

When King Ferdinand returned to his states on this side the Faro, he recalled such as had been exiled for political opinions. Ciro Annichiarico attempted to pass for one of these, and presented himself to the public authorities at Lecce. They gave him a safe conduct to Bari, which was fixed upon as his residence. He pretends that he felt some repentance at this time, and had some idea of shutting himself up in the college of the Missionaries; but being informed that a new order of arrest had been issued against him, he proceeded secretly to Naples, to seek to avert its effects. Soon finding that the attempt was useless, he retired to resume the execrable mode of living which he had not long quitted.

It was about this time that he put himself at the head of the *Patrioti Europei* and *Decisi*. These as-

71   See his Justification at the end of the Memoir.

sociations increased at first, from the weakness of the government in neglecting to punish the guilty, and from the corruption of the lower clergy, and inferior government officers. It was found that priests were attached to all the camps and detachments. The arch-priest, Cirino Cicillo of Cacamola, Vergine of Coregliano, and Leggeri, filled important situations in the sect. The signature of the last was found under the patents, in quality of Captain Reporter, (*Capitano Relatore*). The arch-priest Zurlo, of Valsano, celebrated mass there on Christmas Eve, armed from head to foot.

As soon as these bands had acquired some strength, they sent detachments of resolute men into every town and village. Supported by a larger troop in the neighbourhood, they soon became the despotic masters of insulated places. A horde of twenty or thirty of these ruffians over-ran the country in disguise, masked as Punchinellos."[72] In places where open force could not be employed, the most daring bandits were sent to watch for the moment to execute the sentences of secret death pronounced by the society. It was thus that the Judge of the Peace of Luogo Rotondo and his wife were killed in their own garden, and that the sectary Perone plunged his knife into the bowels of an old man of seventy, dell'Aglio of Francavilla, and afterwards massacred his wife and servant, having introduced himself into their house under pretence of delivering a letter.

---

72 We spare the English reader the enumeration of some of the horrors committed by these ruffians.

They would not suffer neutrality: it was absolutely necessary to join them, or to live exposed to their vengeance, which appeared to be inevitable. They did not invite the support of the rich proprietors and persons of distinction, against whom their hostilities were to be directed, but they unhappily found partisans among the less wealthy; and some of the inferior nobles, who were jealous of the great, also joined them. The government, instead of summoning the opulent proprietors to its assistance, disgusted and offended them by distrust. A meeting at the fair of Galantina to deliberate on the means of checking the disorders, was cried down, and treated at Naples as a revolutionary proceeding. They proved, however, the purity of their intentions, by aiding the government to their utmost, as soon as more energy was shown, and by co-operating with General Church, with whom many individuals of this class served both as officers and private volunteers.

While General Pastore, commandant of these provinces, and the Marquis Predicatella, Intendant of Lecce, inflamed party-spirit by imitating the system of Canosa; the national guard, under their orders, suffered itself to be partly seduced by the sectaries, as well as a number of soldiers and some officers of the crown battalion of reserve.

The number of the sectaries had arrived at its greatest height in the month of December, 1817, and of January, 1818. At that period, they were estimated at 20,000 men. Several of them lived at home, in apparent tranquillity, on the produce of their professions; but they were not the less active in committing unheard-of crimes, as their detection was more difficult. Persons have been known to sign, under their poignards, contracts for the sale of their houses or lands, the objects of the avarice of these ruffians; these contracts were executed in all the forms of law, and acknowledgements were given by the owners for sums which they had never received.

The Lodges of the Decided (*i Decisi*) were called Decisions (*Decisioni*)—the Assemblies of the Reformed European Patriots, Squadrons (*Squadriglie*), each from forty to sixty strong; and those of the Philadelphes, Camps (*Campi*), about three or four hundred strong. There were one hundred and thirteen Camps and Squadrons in the province of Lecce, and four in the city of that name. The organization of these Camps and Squadrons was military; we find in them a President Commandant, two Counsellors, two Captains, an Aide-de-Camp, a Captain Reporter, a Secretary, a Keeper of the Seals, &c. &c. Their sittings were at first held in the night, and carefully guarded by sentinels; their military exercises took place in solitary houses, or suppressed and deserted convents; but taking courage by degrees, they were afterwards seen performing their evolutions by day, and in the open air. Many of them had fire-arms, almost all had poignards. They began at the same time to organize a corps of cavalry. On the day appointed for the great revolution, Ciro had promised to furnish horses to two hundred armed conspirators of Francavilla, who were to repair, on the 27th of February, 1818, to a certain place near S. Marzano. It appears that the engagement was kept on neither side, for in the very prison of Francavilla, Ciro, and some conspirators of that town, mutually reproached each other with having betrayed their cause by neglecting this agreement.

The Institution of the Decided, or *Decisi*, is so horrible that it makes one shudder. The patent given at the end of this Memoir, and transcribed and commented on here, will give some idea of the Society.[73]

S. (Salentina) D. (Decisione)
S. (Salute)

No. 5. Uo. Mazoni Grandi, (Muratori Grandi)
L. D. D. T. G. S. A. F. G. C. I. T. D. U. &c.
La Decisione del Tonante Giove (name of the Lodge or Decisipn) *spera a fare Guerra contro i Tiranni dell' Universo, &c.*

> (*The Initials and the letters printed in red, are written with blood in the original.*)

Il mortale Gaetano Caffieri e un F. D. (Fratello Deciso) No. cinque, appartenente alia De. (Decisione) del Giove Tonante sparsa sulla superficie della Terra; per la sua De. (Decisione) ha avuto

---

73   See the Plate.

il piacere di fare parte in questa R. S. D. (Repub-licana Salentina Decisione). Noi dunque invitia-mo tutte le Societa filantropiche a prestare il loro braccio forte al medesimo ed a soccorrerlo nei suoi bisogni, essendo egli giunto alia De. (Deci-sione) di acquistare la liberta o morte. Oggi li 29 Ottobre, 1817.

Signed,

Pietro Gargaro, II G. M. D. No. 1.
. . . .
(II Gran Mastro Deciso, No. 1 .)
V. de Serio, 2°. Deciso.
Gaetano CAFFIERI.
Registratore dei Morti.

* * *

TRANSLATION.

*The Salentine Decision
Health*

No. 5, Grand Masons.

The Decision of Jupiter the Thunderer hopes to make war against the tyrants of the universe, &c. &c.

The mortal Gaetano Caffieri is a Brother Decid-ed, No. 5. belonging to the Decision of Jupiter the Thunderer, spread over the face of the Earth, by his Decision, has had the pleasure to belong to this Salentine Republican Decision. We invite, therefore, all Philanthropic Societies to lend their strong arm to the same, and to assist him in his wants, he having come to the Decision he will obtain liberty or death. Dated this day the 29th of October, 1817.

Signed,

Pietro GARGARO (the Decided Grand
.... Master, No. 1 .)
Vito de Serio, Second Decided.
Gaetano CAFFIERI,
Registrar of the Dead.

*** * *

As the number of these Decided ruffians was small, they easily recognised each other. We find that the Grand Master bears the No. 1.; Vito de Serio, No. 2; the proprietor of the patent, Gaetano Caffieri, No. 5. He figures himself among the signatures with the title of Registrar of the Dead, which does not allude to the deceased members of the Society, but to the victims they immolated, and of whom they kept a register apart, on the margin of which were found blasphemies and infernal projects. They had also a Director of Funeral Ceremonies, for they slaughtered with method and solemnity. As soon as the detachments employed on this service found it convenient to effect their purpose, at the signal of the first blast of a trumpet they unsheathed their poignards; they aimed them at their victim at the second blast; at the third they gradually approach their weapons to his breast "*con vero entusiasmo*" (with real enthusiasm), in their cannibal language, and plunged them into his body at the fourth signal.

The four points which are observable after the signature of Pietro Gargaro, indicate his power of passing sentence of death. When the Decisi wrote to any one to extort contributions, or to command him to do any thing—if they added these four points, it was known that the person they addressed was condemned to death in case of disobedience. If the points were not added, he was threatened with milder punishment, such as laying waste his fields, or burning his house.

The Salentine Republic, the ancient name of this district, was also that destined for their imaginary Republic, which they called "*un anello della Republica Europea*," a link of the European Republic.

The symbols of the Thunderbolt darting from a cloud and striking the crowns and tiara; the Fasces and the Cap of Liberty planted upon a death's head between two axes; the skulls and bones with the words "*Tristezza, Morte, Terrore, e Lutto*," Sadness, Death, Terror, and Mourning, sufficiently characterize this Association. Their colours were yellow, red, and blue, which surround the patent.

It is dated according to the common style, 29th of October, 1817, while those of the Philadelphes and Reformed European Patriots, which are also given at the end, have an æra of their own; the first is dated Lecce, the 15th of March, third year, which corresponds with the year 1816, and the second "Lecce, at the camp of Avenged Liberty, fifth year," that is to say, in 1817.

The fees required for these certificates formed a branch of the revenue of the Society, as well as the forced contributions in money and provisions.

Such were the excesses which accompanied these disorders, when it was at last considered time at Naples to put an end to them. In the summer of 1817, General Church was sent to Lecce to reconnoitre the country, and the state of things; some months afterwards, he was entrusted with the command of the provinces of Bari and Otranto, and General Pastore was recalled. The Intendant Predicatella was superseded in his functions for a time, by the Secretary-General Amanti. General Church, armed with the royal Alter-Ego, or, in other words, with full and unlimited powers, passed the Ofanto with 1200 men of the foreign regiments in the Neapolitan service, formed by himself; among them were some companies of cavalry. He could depend upon these soldiers, the greater part of whom were Germans, Swiss, and Albanians. Those who were in the country, were only to be depended upon, after having witnessed the firm determination with which the General set about the enterprize, and after the factious individuals had been weeded out. It was the same with the militia.

The ready co-operation of the wealthy proprietors has been already noticed. The Dukes of Cesareo and of Monte Jasi were the most zealous. Encouraged by their example, several individuals, even of the lowest class, furnished information concerning the criminals. The fear of not being supported had prevented them from doing so before; but the greatest part of the latter description were silent, and maintained a line of conduct which indicated that they would not hesitate to declare for the sectaries, if the latter should succeed in eluding the efforts of the new General, as they had done those of his predecessors. This was particularly the case in the neighbourhood of Tarentum, at Grottaglie, S. Marzano, Martina, and Francavilla, the usual haunts of Ciro and his friends. When General Church first visited these places, the inhabitants looked on in gloomy silence, and no person saluted him; a poor monk was the only person who bowed to him.

The bandits and the banished (*fuorusciti e fuorbanditi*) were summoned ineffectually for the last time, before the Royal Commission at Lecce, instituted by the decree of the 17th of July, 1817. Ciro Annichiarico sent the Justification annexed to this Memoir. General Church made his military dispositions. He divided his troops into moveable columns sufficiently strong, and only placed garrisons upon some points which were absolutely essential; either from their commanding the vast plains of that country, or because they were strong enough to serve as places of retreat for the brigands. The ground offered little difficulty in beating and traversing in all directions, but it was extensive compared to the number of the troops, and exposed them to constant fatigue, which, however, they supported without a murmur, encouraged by the example of their chief and officers, and well fed and paid. The moveable columns all operated towards a common centre, by gradually narrowing the circle, in the middle of which were the towns of Grottaglie, S. Marzano, and Francavilla. Other columns of reserve accompanied the General, who proceeded wherever the spies had traces of Ciro Annichiarico.

"*È un altro Uomo quello Generaledai precedenti che m'hanno mandati sul corpo,*" said Ciro, biting his thumb, in token of rage and disappointment: "*ho b—— tanti Generali, Francesi, Italiani, e Napolitani, ma quello finisce a b—— mi a me.*" "This General is another sort of man from those whom they sent against me before. I have made fools of many Generals, French, Italian, and Neapolitans, but this one will end by making a fool of me."

He soon perceived that he lost resources daily, that his credit was weakened, and that those who were still faithful to him would probably turn their backs upon him. He had a proof of their fickleness, when, despairing of success, he attempted to embark at Brindisi. The captain of the vessel recognised him, and dem anded 2000 ducats as the price of his safety; not having them to give, he wrote to his friends, who refused to advance the sum.

Pressed and surrounded more and more closely, Ciro resolved to risk a general rising and a pitched battle. He fixed the 27th of February for this purpose, and appointed the place of rendezvous under the walls of S. Marzano, but his catastrophe took place before that time.

S. Marzano, an Albanian colony, is a miserable little village, containing from 900 to 1000 inhabitants, belonging to the Marquis Bonelli, of Barletta, and situated some miles distant from the road between Manduria and Tarentum. It is admirably calculated for a military position, the rocky hill on which the town is built, and which is planted with olives, is surrounded and intersected by garden walls; it is quite insulated and extends from east to west. The view from the terrace of the baronial castle is magnificent. From this spot, the town of Oria and the towers of Francavilla are discerned, and in another direction Monte Asole and Grottaglie.

It was from the latter place that Ciro Annichiarico set out, on the 25th of January, 1818, with forty horsemen and ten foot; when at two o'clock in the afternoon he fell in with a detachment of cavalry consisting of eighteen men, commanded by Captain Montori, who charged him, and drove him as far as Neviera, a farm at the foot of the hill of S. Marzano. He there made some resistance, and afterwards retreated into the town itself. Captain Montori attempted to enter by the steep and narrow path which wound up to it, but Ciro Annichiarico and his adherents of S. Marzario posted themselves on an elevated point and repulsed him. He turned the hill in order to scale it on the side of Manduria, but there, too, he was received by a shower of balls. He observed, however, that they were the same men who had followed his movements, and hence concluded that they were not strong enough to defend all the points at once, and that he should gain his object by deceiving them. Concealed by the wall of a garden, he attracted the enemy by firing a carbine or two on one side, while he suddenly hastened with the rest of his men to the other. This stratagem succeeded: Montori entered S. Marzano, and the panic-struck followers of Ciro dispersed. Ciro himself effected his escape, Captain Montori not having men enough to guard the passes. Immediately afterwards, the infantry of the moveable column arrived. A census of the town was taken, the Mayor suggested to Major Bianchi of the National Guard a method of discovering the delinquents. Every house was searched, and the guilty were recognized by the smell or the blackness of their hands, a proof of their having recently handled fire-arms and powder. Vito Serio, the brothers Francesco and Angelo Vito Lecce, Raffaello Zaccharia, and Pietro Barbuzzi were arrested, and all executed, on the 3d of February, at Francavilla. Their heads were placed before the church of S. Marzano, which was blown down by a hurricane some months afterwards, and they were buried beneath its ruins. On this occasion the black standard and decorations of Ciro were taken. General Church sent them to Naples, and they were presented to the King by Prince Nugent, the Captain-General. Major Bianchi followed up the advantage that had been gained. The next day he proceeded to Francavilla. He there found the inhabitants in great fermentation, determined to break open the prisons and release those confined in them. Having ascertained who were the ringleaders, he lost not a moment in causing them to be seized in their houses. He sent his gendarmes into the streets with orders to lay hands on all they should meet in arms. This daring measure terrified the people, and fully succeeded in quelling the tumult.

The troops drew nearer Francavilla; a military commission was established there to try the offenders. General Church arrived in person. Knowing that Ciro could not be very far distant, and that he had the most intimate correspondence with S. Marzano, he threatened that town with pillage as a punishment for its rebellious conduct, unless it enabled him to secure the person of Ciro within eight days. Trembling for their property, the militia undertook to pursue him. On the 5th or 6th of February, the militia of S. Marzano learnt that Ciro had thrown himself into the farm-house (Masseria) of Scaserba, belonging to the chapter of Grottaglie, at about ten miles from Francavilla.

The Masserie in Apulia and the provinces of Otranto and Tarentum are all built on the same plan, and are capable of defence; the word is not altogether rendered by "farm-house," which gives but an inadequate idea of the Masseria. They date from the period when the incursions of the Turks and pirates were apprehended, and when the country people shut themselves up in their holds with their cattle and most valuable effects, in order to secure themselves from a sudden attack. A square wall of enclosure, sufficiently high and solid, generally surrounds the dwelling-house, built against one side, and containing two or three habitable rooms, and sometimes a small chapel, the asylum for culprits—"*Qui non si gode asilo*," (Here no sanctuary is enjoyed) informs them if this privilege is not attached to it. The stables and out-houses form a right angle with this dwellinghouse; but without touching it. At some distance from the surrounding wall, rises a round or square tower of two stories, standing quite alone. The ascent to the first story is either by stone steps inserted in the tower, by a drawbridge, or by a ladder easily drawn up. This was the case in the Masseria of Scaserba, the plan of which is here given.

Plan of the Masseria of Scaserba, last place of retreat of Ciro Annichiarico.

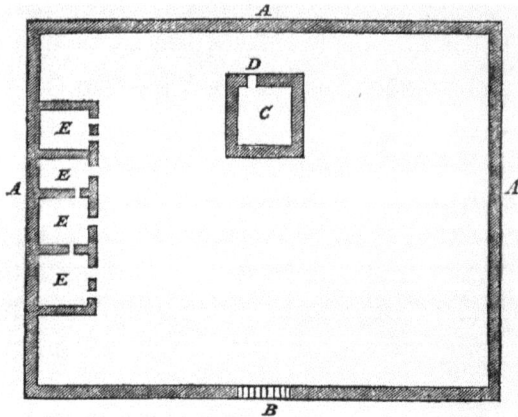

A. A. A. Wall of enclosure.
B. Large entrance gate.
C. Square insulated tower.
D. Door of the tower.
E. E. E. E. Granaries and stables.

Worn out with fatigue, Ciro and three companions, Vito di Cesare, Giovanni Palmieri, and Michele Cuppoli, had taken refuge in Scaserba, to repose themselves for a few hours. He had previously provided this and all the farm-houses of the district with ammunition and some provisions. When he saw the militia of S. Marzano marching against him, he appeared very little alarmed, and thought he could easily cut his way through their ranks. He shot the first man dead who came within range of his musket. This delay cost him dear: the militia sent information to Lieutenant Fonsmorte, stationed at the "Castelli," a strong position between Grottaglie and Francavilla. This officer hastened to the spot with forty men. On seeing him approach, perceived that a vigorous attack was to be made. He shut up the people of the Masseria in the straw magazine, and put the key in his pocket. He took away the ladder from the tower, and loaded, with the aid of his companions, all the guns, of which he had a good number.

Major Bianchi, informed of what was going on, sent on the same evening a detachment of Gendarmes, under Captain Corsi, and the next morning proceeded in person to Scaserba. The siege was formed by 132 soldiers; the militia, on which little dependence was placed, were stationed at some distance, and in the second line. Ciro vigorously defended the approaches to his tower till sun-set. He attempted to escape in the night, but the neighing of a horse made him suspect that some cavalry had arrived, whose pursuit it would be impossible to elude. He retired, after having killed, with a pistol shot, a Voltigeur, stationed under the wall he had attempted to scale. He again shut himself up in his tower, and employed himself till morning in making cartridges. At day-break, the besiegers tried to burst open the wooden gate of the outer wall; Ciro and his men repulsed the assailants by a well-directed fire, they killed five and wounded fourteen men. A barrel of oil was brought in order to burn the door. The first man who set fire to it was shot through the heart. A four pounder which had been conveyed to the place was pointed against the roof of the tower. Several of this calibre had been contrived to be easily dismounted from their carriages, and transported on mules. This little piece produced great effect. The tiles and bricks which fell, forced Ciro to descend from the second story to the first. He was tormented with a burning thirst, for he had forgotten to provide himself with water, and he never drank wine. This thirst soon became insupportable.

After some deliberations with his companions, he demanded to speak with General Church, who he believed was in the neighbourhood, then to the Duke of Jasi, who was also absent; at last he resolved to capitulate with Major Bianchi. He addressed the besiegers, and threw them some bread. Major Bianchi promised him that he should not be maltreated by the soldiers. He descended the ladder, opened the door of the tower, and presented himself with the words *"Eccomi, Don Ciro!"*—Here I am, Don Ciro!

He begged them to give him some water to quench his thirst, and desired them to liberate the farmer and his family, who had been shut up all this while in the straw magazine. He declared that they were innocent, and distributed money among them.

He suffered himself to be searched and bound patiently; some poison was found upon him; he asserted that his companions had prevented him from taking it. He conversed quietly enough with

Major Bianchi on the road to Francavilla, and related to him the principal circumstances of his life.

In prison, he appeared to be interested for the fate of some of his partisans, begging that they might not be persecuted, and declaring that they had been forced to do what they had done.

He had entertained some hope, till the moment when he was placed before the Council of War, under the direction of Lieutenant-Colonel Guarini. He addressed a speech to him, taking him for General Church. He insisted on speaking to. that officer; this was refused, and he resigned himself to his fate, drily saying, "*Ho capito,*" (I understand —).

When condemned to death, a Missionary offered him the consolations of religion, Ciro answered him with a smile, "*Lasciate queste chiacchiere; siamo dell'istessa professione; non ci burliamo fra noi.*"—Let us leave alone this prating; we are of the same profession; don't let us laugh at one another.

As he was led to execution, the 8th of February, 1818, he recognised Lieutenant Fonsmorte, and addressed these words to him, "*Se io fosse Re, vi farei Capitano,*"—If I were King I would make you a Captain. This officer was the first to arrive at Scaserba with his soldiers.

The streets of Francavilla were filled with people: there were spectators even upon the roofs. They all preserved a gloomy silence.

On his arrival at the place of execution, Ciro wished to remain standing, he was told to kneel, he did so, presenting his breast. He was then informed that malefactors, like himself, were shot with their backs towards the soldiers; he submitted, at the same time advising a priest, who persisted in remaining near him, to withdraw, so as not to expose himself.

Twenty-one balls took effect, four in the head, yet he still breathed and muttered in his throat; the twenty-second put an end to him. This fact is confirmed by all the officers and soldiers present at his death. "As soon as we perceived," said a soldier, very gravely, "that he was enchanted, we loaded his own musket with a silver ball, and this destroyed the spell."[74] It will be easily supposed that the people, who always attributed supernatural powers to him, were confirmed in their belief by this tenaciousness of life, which they considered miraculous.

On the following day, the 9th of February, ten of the most criminal among the Decisi were executed at Francavilla, among whom were all the dignitaries whose signatures are contained in the patent given at the end.

They were led through the streets of Francavilla; several of them recognized, at the windows, the fathers, the sons, or the relations of those whom they had assassinated, and asked pardon of

74 It is still believed in Scotland, that Viscount Dundee, commonly known by the name of Graham of Claverhouse, was invulnerable to all ordinary weapons, and that his death, at the battle of Killiecrankie, was owing to the presence of mind of a young officer, who, finding himself within pistol shot of Dundee, twisted a silver button off his jacket, with which he loaded his piece and shot the Viscount through the heart. —T.

them. But these were the only ones who expressed the least feeling of repentance. All the others were so hardened and fanatical, that they died without regretting their crimes, and with a ferocious indifference.

The military tribunal afterwards brought about 227 persons to trial; nearly half of them, having been guilty of murder and robbery by force of arms, were condemned to capital punishment, and their heads were exposed near the places of their residence, or in the scene of their crimes.

In a short time, peace was restored to these desolated provinces. General Church used his power with discretion. His established principle was to listen to, or receive no accusation against political opinions, or connexions with secret societies; but he punished crimes and deeds of violence with severity. He caused the accused to be tried without delay; expelled vagrants; and dismissed from their situations such government officers as could not be depended upon. Instead of seizing the arms without an equivalent, he caused their value to be paid. He threatened with death such artisans as should dare to manufacture prohibited arms. He exhorted the confessors to endeavour to get possession of the poignards, or to oblige the penitents to throw them into wells.

The city of Lecce, grateful for the blessing of restored tranquillity, voted a statue to the King, and a sword of honour, with the freedom of the city, to General Church.

The following are extracts from the several publications and circulars of the Field-Marshal, Plenipotentiary Commissioner of the King, addressed to the authorities of the provinces of Lecce and Otranto, to efface even the traces of the impression which these scenes of horror had produced there.

General Church to the Syndics, &c.

Head-Quarters, Lecce,
20th September, 1818.

1. H. M. the   has commanded the publication of an act of perfect amnesty as to the past, as far as regards the criminal associations held in different parts of the province by some persons who attempt to mislead the people. The act of H. M. comprehends all those who, from ignorance or fear, have consented to belong to these associations, it being well understood that they have returned to the straight line of duty.

The General having made a report to the King on the tranquillity which reigned in his division, and on the dissolution of the sects, H. M. declares, through him, that he no longer believes in the existence of such associations.

2. Persons imprisoned, exiles, or fugitives, as well as those guilty of assassination, or ordinaiy crimes, are not comprehended in this amnesty.

3. After this declaration of the sovereign, the General, commanding this sixth military division, publicly announces that he will receive no accusation against the individuals of this province, on the subject of the principal or secondary part which they may be accused of having taken in the unfortunate events of the province.

4. The King: thanks all those who have contributed to the establishment of good order.

A proclamation of the month of April, 1819, directs all the Local Authorities who, till then, had addressed their reports directly to the General, to send them in future to their ordinary superiors, as they did before these troubles.

Lastly, a letter dated Lecce, 28th of April, 1810, contains the following dispositions:

> The reign of the assassins being at an end, and all the province tranquillized, it is resolved, in order to extinguish their memory, that the heads of the malefactors executed in pursuance of the sentences of the military commission, and which are exposed under the church towers, and other parts of the town, shall be taken down and interred, and that the places where they were exposed shall be entirely cleaned and white-washed. This letter shall be read by the Arch-priests in all the churches.

The death of Ciro and his principal accomplices happily put an end to disturbances which had threatened to take a wider range. The following Justification, which Ciro sent to Lecce, in answer to the summons addressed to him, will complete the portrait of this audacious robber captain, who was not altogether destitute of those talents which most impose upon the multitude.

* * *

JUSTIFICATION OF CIRO ANNICHIARICO.

To the Commission assembled by the Royal Decree of the 17th of July, 1817.

The Priest Ciro Annichiarico, of the town of Grottaglie, has learnt with surprize that the commission appointed in Lecce for the purpose of launching the thunders of exile against those who range the country in arms, committing excesses, and resisting the public force, demands the reason why Ciro Annichiarico lives out of his country. At the same time the definitive sentence of exile is threatened to be passed, unless within the space of eight days, the relations or friends of the accused explain to the Commission the reason of his non-appearance.

It is not to be hoped, Most Respectable Signers, that any person can be found to undertake the defence of Annichiarico, since the fear of the soldiers, who would mark such a person out for destruction, prevents even his nearest relations from lending the succour they owe, to one belongs to them by every tie of nature and of blood. I am, therefore, obliged to make my own defence, which I write in a gloomy forest (*dalla piu orrida foresta*), that is at once my home and my sanctuary. I write it with boldness of heart, for I feel within me no tumult which reproaches me with having ever acted against reason, or with having in the slightest degree oifended against the sacred laws of virtue, of probity, and of honour. At this moment I appeal to your own unsullied justice, and am quite certain that, having laid aside all prejudice and passion, your generous, wise, and well-formed hearts will be penetrated with compassion for one who, till this moment, has been, through misrepresentation, the object of hatred and execration.

In the year 1803, the murder committed on the body of Giuseppe, son of the late Nicola Motolese, was imputed to me. At that time the town of Grottaglie was divided by two parties, which are always the cause of private and public ruin. I was supposed to belong to one of these, for which reason the above imputation was cast upon me by the opposite faction. The government which then regulated the province of Lecce began to persecute my innocent brothers without ceasing, expecting them to deliver up their own brother. Trusting in my innocence, and induced by fraternal love, I instantly flew to present myself to the extraordinary commission of Apulia sitting at Trani. That assembly being dissolved, I was handed over to Lecce to be tried by the ordinary tribunal. It was to me a most fearful instance of the intrigues of power; for without defence, without a possibility of obtaining permission to extend the very limited time allowed for trial, and, as I was told, even without the consent of my feeble counsel; my cause was perverted, I became the victim of imposture, and was sentenced to fifteen years of exile. For four successive years I was kept in the most dreadful of prisons, without being sent to my destination, notwithstanding the repeated petitions which I sent to the ministers of justice. I at last succeeded in escaping, by eluding the vigilance of my keepers. I found myself free, it is true, but every effort, every possible intrigue was employed to arrest me. From that moment, the most cruel and incessant persecutions were begun, even to attempting my death by a black scheme of treachery to which my innocent brother fell a victim, and by which I was severely wounded. For a long time I was obliged to live in a wretched state, in remote solitudes, and my existence differed in nothing from that of savages and wild beasts. The most gloomy caverns formed my retreat, and in constant want of the merest necessaries for human sustenance, I passed my days amidst the horrors of the forests and of the rocks. I sometimes obtained a scanty meal from the pity of the keepers of the flocks; and the wild fruits of mother earth often supplied me with the means of satisfying hunger. All that remained with me was my invincible courage, and the peace of a conscience which reproached me with nothing. In the mean time, disturbances took place in various parts of the province, and the blame was always unjustly made to fall upon me. Whatever robbery, whatever murder, whatever assassination[75] was committed on the face of the earth, was instantly given out by the cabal to be owing to the Abbate Annichiarico. The very offenders themselves, either to conceal their own names or to excuse their iniquitous actions, have implicated no name but that of the Abbate Annichiarico. And why have they not said that the wars, fomented by cruel ambition, to the destruction of miserable human beings—why have they not said that these also were kindled by the Abbate Annichiarico? In consequence of such accusation, without proofs, because all were false, the government of the military occupation[76] declared me without the pale of the laws.

My innocent brothers, sent for the second time to the prisons of Lecce, suffered for many months a punishment which they had done nothing to deserve; while their families, abandoned, and destitute of all human succour, languished in the greatest misery. These, indeed, would have been circumstances sufficient to drive me to every excess, had not the Almighty (*il grande Architetto dell'universo*), by his timely assistance, revived in my heart the sentiments of religion.

---

75 (*qualunque assassinamento*): *assassinamento* means strictly a high-way robbery. The brigands are called *assassini*. —Ed.

76 "*L'occupazione militare*," the term appropriated to Murat's government.

In the mean time, the arms of the Bourbons re-entered the kingdom, and the glorious reigning monarch benignly resolved to recal into the order of society all those who had been banished from it. Among the rest, I sought to profit by the beneficent determination of the sovereign, and therefore presented myself to the authorities at Lecce. The government favoured my wishes, I obtained a temporary safe conduct, I was fixed at Bari under the inspection of the police, and the most pleasing hopes were kindled within me, of seeing myself for once at rest, living without fear, in society and order. It was then that I examined myself and called to mind my duties. I reflected seriously on the indelible obligations imposed on me by my sacred profession, and I determined to retire to the College of the Missionaries at Bari, with the permission of the usual minister employed for this purpose by the Eccellentissimo Capece Latro, Archbishop of Tarentum. I was on the point of following up my noble resolution, when the thunderbolt burst upon my head (*allorchè intesi lo scroscio del violentissimo fulmine, che si scagliava sul mio capo*). Ah! let it be permitted me, most respectable Signors, to exclaim this moment with Æneas, (*coll'Enea di Virgilio*)—"*Infandum—jubete vos—renovare dolorem.*" I have not force enough to express to you how my heart was rent, or the deplorable state which I miserably sunk into, when I was secretly informed by a faithful friend, that my arrest was ordered on the cruel accusation of having infringed the mandate. I vanished like lightning from Bari; I went to the capital to obtain redress, and to discover once more the black conspiracy against me. All was vain. The hopes I had cherished, disappeared; and while perplexed as to the steps I ought to take, the power of my relentless persecutors prevailed. At last I left the capital, and guided only by that fortitude and constancy so necessary in my misfortunes, I betook myself to my old haunts in the solitude of the forests, and recommenced a savage and wretched life.

In this miserable state, circumstances invited me to crimes and vengeance; but the feelings of nature and religion within me recalled me to duty. After some time, I learnt with horror from the charitable shepherds, that a set of brigands infested the Apennines that lie between Martina and Grottaglie my native town. I was told that husbandmen had abandoned their farms, flocks and herds, and the labours of the field, to fly from repeated incursions of these assassins. I was informed of the robberies and outrages committed on passengers, and I felt my heart bleed (*spezzare*) when these disasters happened, and especially when my townsmen were the victims. A better opportunity could not, certainly, present itself to an irritated man, to improve his miserable state, by joining this horde of robbers. But I felt just the reverse: I conceived in my mind the noble idea of succouring mankind. This thought raised within me the pleasing hope of being one day able to un-deceive the government, as to the calumnies that were heaped upon me. I therefore issued from my cavern with courage, and forsaking the deep forest that had been my home, I at last arrived at the road to Martina in the Apennines. I forbear to disclose what happened afterwards; suffice it to say, and I can say it with truth, that these roads through the Apennines are free, the traveller journeys without dread, the farm-houses are re-opened, and the shepherd sings while he leads his peaceful flock to pasture.

Such, most noble Signors, is the faithful narrative of the actions of the priest Ciro Annichiarico. I hve at a distance from my dear country, because the government will not receive me into society and order: I fly my father's house, because the seizure of my person and my death are meditated. Treachery has confined me to the woods, and deprives me of human intercourse. If the government of the province had not been so precipitate, in lending faith to calumny, I should certainly be enjoying my natural and civil liberty; and I should at this moment be in the bosom of my family, or at least I should continue to live at Bari, under the inspection of the police. I should at any rate be living in order, and I too should taste the sweets and blessings of society. Thus have I myself assigned the reason of my absence, which was asked of my relations and friends. The Commission has, however, declared me out of the protection of the law, and has threatened to pass the definitive sentence against me. Let me be permitted to ask, in one word, what are my offences? Just those that are falsely attributed to me by my adversaries, those that are the offspring of cabal and imposture, those that are brought forward by culprits in custody, who, either corrupted by intrigue, or secretly flattering themselves that they may escape punishment, have been induced to name the Abbate Annichiarico. And do these deserve to be believed? and are these the grounds of my banishment? and is it thus that your incorruptible (*incorrotta*) justice, most excellent Signors, is induced to heap the most opprobrious punishment upon a citizen, in whose breast the sincerest sentiments of honour and virtue are engraved? upon a man who, with the warmest feehngs of charity, has been ready to shed his blood to aid his fellow-creatures, by snatching them from the fangs (*branche*) of bandits? —Have I ever resisted in arms the public force? Have I ever ranged the country in arms for the purposes of robbery, and to load myself with crimes? If such actions had ever been committed by me, I should certainly not find a hand charitable enough to prolong my life, and the earth itself would not afford me an asylum from destruction.

Ah! most gentle Signors, why will you drive me to desperation, and to crimes which my heart so much abhors! Why seek the total ruin of a man, of an honest citizen, of a priest, of a faithful friend to public order? At this moment I appeal to your rigid justice;—you, who cherish in your breasts the sentiments of pity, exert yourselves, at length, in favour of an unhappy being, miserably oppressed and persecuted for the long space of fifteen years; make an energetic representation to the Sovereign, that permission may be granted me to return to society, and to live in the discharge of my sacred duties. I see the abyss that threatens to swallow me up; I foresee the series of evils and crimes into which I may be compelled: I shudder at the prospect. Spare me, for pity's sake, this sad catastrophe of misfortunes, and lend assistance to one whose Hfe is passed in the gloomy solitude of the forest, and the loathsomeness of the cavern.

THE PRIEST CIRO ANNICHIARICO.

The 6th November, 1817.

Conclusion

Letter from the
Author to the Translator

Naples, Jan. 25th, 1821.

SIR,

I trust this letter will reach you in time to be inserted at the end of the *Memoirs of the Carbonari*, as it contains some facts in support of the opinions already advanced as to the natural progress of the sect, if not disturbed by external force.

A pamphlet[1] which appeared about a month

---

1   *Memoria del Avvocato D. Carlo Quarto, nella Causa dei tre Arrestati Guglielmo Paladini, Salvatore Vecchiarelli e Pasquale Maenza, colla Decisione della Gran Corte Criminale di*

ago, in defence of G. Paladini, S. Vecchiarelli, and P. Maenza, proves, that, from the month of August, 1820, that is to say, shortly after the revolution of Naples, the Carbonari were divided into two distinct parties: the first may be called, that of the Constitutional Carbonari, who considered their labours ended, and their object obtained, on the establishment of a constitutional government. The second, or Ultra Carbonari, redoubled their zeal at that period; and had it not been for the opposition of the others, they would, undoubtedly, have forced the revolution of their country to run through all the changes of that of France, and have hurried it as soon as possible into a reign of terror. At the time when the Austrian reinforcements had begun to assemble in Lombardy, when the Prince of Cariato had been sent back from Vienna, and Palermo was in a state of insurrection, men of sense perceived that nothing could avert the storm but moderate conduct, and carefully avoiding the horrors which have hitherto been but the too faithful attendants on popular insurrections.

With these intentions, they endeavoured to gain the Carbonari, to which order they belonged, and contrived to win over the Supreme Lodge of Naples, whose president, Giuliano, had formerly been a police officer; and also some of the provincial magistracies.

Napoli; si aggiunge una Leggenda delle Operazloni combinate per formare e sostenere la Calunnia, ed un Indirizzo di Accusa al Parlamenta contro i Calunniatori.

But their views were displeasing to the Ultra Carbonari, whose doctrine it was, that blood must cement all revolutions, and that it was impossible to answer for their partizans, unless they implicated them in the commission of crimes, to cut off all hope of retreat. They raised the cry of imbecility and treason, and demanded vigorous measures Several provincial lodges hastened to send deputies to Naples, in order to stir up the Carbonaro populace, and to arm it tumultuously. But, whether it was that the deputies acquitted themselves imperfectly of their commission, or that the Committee of Public Safety, with Borelli at its head, had counteracted them effectually; they were but coldly received.

But the ultras of the capital were not disheartened at this first repulse: they, on their part, despatched emissaries into the provinces. Paladini, Vecchiarelli and Maenza, were of the number: they went to Salerno on the 2d September, thence to Avellino on the 5th, and came back to Naples on the night between the 5th and 6th; they were arrested in their carriage, in the Square of La Carita.

It appears that letters from the Governor and from the General Commandant of Avellino gave the first alarm concerning their mission. They were accused of "attempting to stir up sedition in the three provinces, Naples, Salerno, and Avellino in order to overturn the high government authorities; and of conspiring against the sacred persons of the King and other members of the Royal Family."[2] The suspicions against them were increased, by their destroying their papers the moment they were arrested.

After passing sixty-seven days imprisoned in the Castles of St. Elmo and Del' Ovo, the persons accused were dismissed by the ordinary tribunals to which this cause had been referred, for want of proof.

Meantime the Jacobine lodges, though forming but a slender minority, continue their dark intrigues. Their members, interdicted and rejected from all community with the others, bear the name of Solitary or Dispersed Greeks, *i Greci solitari o dispersi*. The lodge of the Pythagoreans, whose oath has been given in the body of the work, as well as the acts of the third rank of Carbonari, which we mentioned as an anomaly in the sect, appear to bear reference to them. A short time ago, Lucente, the Governor of Teramo, caused their lodges to be shut up. It is these Dispersed Greeks who have filled many peaceable persons with such terror, that they do not think themselves safe from their violence at any time or place, and who have alarmed the minds even of the most august personages, although they have hitherto been watched with sufficient vigilance to prevent their attempting any serious outrage.

The excellent constitution of the National Guard, Guardia di Sicurezza, of the capital, formed as it is of proprietors interested in the maintenance

---

2   Memorial of the Advocate D. C. Quarto, p. 3.

of order, has greatly facilitated the means of doing this. The Neapolitan legions, on the contrary, composed of the classes in less easy circumstances, and of which almost every soldier is a Carbonaro, represent the most turbulent party. Behind-hand in discipline as in dress, they are not in habits of cordiality with the National Guard, and still less with the Royal Guard, who are believed to incline towards the Calderari.

These misunderstandings broke out openly a few days since, on occasion of the suspending veto of the Prince Regent pronounced upon certain modifications of the Spanish constitution, relative to religion. The veto had been instigated by the violent remonstrance of Cardinal Ruffo, Archbishop of Naples, and of twenty-two of the other archbishops and bishops of the kingdom.

On the 15th January, some hundreds of persons, said to belong to the legions and to the violent lodges, assembled in the Court of Parliament, and took possession of the tribunes. They had the impudence to address the deputies, and to demand the punishment of the Cardinal Archbishop; the adoption of the modifications, in defiance of the veto; the dissolution of the Committee of Public Safety; and the reduction of the Royal Guard.

The reproaches, however, of the popular deputies, who taxed them with having sold themselves to some foreign power, in order to dishonour the nation, sufficed to silence and disperse the mob. But the same evening, skirmishes between the legionaries and the National Guard, took place in several quarters of the city: happily, the latter were uniformly successful; and we are assured, that a reform in the legions of the capital, and a purging of the lodges, in order to get rid of the unavowed members, will be the consequence, and that they have already begun, by withdrawing and burning some thousands of patents which had been granted to Carbonari of that kind.

The war which threatens the Kingdom of the Two Sicilies, and which the sects have in some measure drawn upon it, makes the constitutional Carbonari exert themselves to the utmost, to efface from their association the character of a secret society, and to impress it with that of an institution for the maintenance of the present order of things, which they look upon as their own work.

It is on this consideration, that Don G. Troyse, Minister of Pardon and Justice, addressed a circular letter to the higher clergy, in order to convince them, that the Papal bulls refusing absolution after confession to the members of secret societies, are no longer applicable to the Carbonari:[3]

"It is time," he says,

> to abjure the errors into which we had fallen with regard to these societies, whose object is no longer a mystery, because they are so widely

---

3   *Circolare del Ministro di Giustizia e Grazie, agli III^mo e Riv^mi Arcivescovi, Vescovi, &c. del 23 Dec. 1820. Napoli. Signat.* II Ministro degli Affai Ecclesiastici,

G. Troyse.

extended that no class of citizens can now be ignorant of the purposes of their meetings. They
laboured to obtain that constitution, which was
solemnly acknowledged and sworn to by his
Majesty—that constitution, which, by its twelfth
article, acknowledges no religion but that of the
Roman, Catholic and Apostolic Church, professed by our fathers, and which shall always be
ours.

Now is it not wilfully diminishing the respect
due to the Holy See, when we attribute to it
power matters merely political, and completely
foreign to its province? All mystery being now
laid aside, and the object of the Carbonari openly avowed, their societies are no longer subject
to the bulls in any way, but are amenable directly and exclusively to the laws of the realm.

With regard to the occurrences at Lecce, in 1817,
&c. of which I have placed the particulars after the
account of the Carbonari, you will do well to turn
your attention to the debates of the Neapolitan
Parliament, on the 3d of January, 1821.

The deputy Arcovito brought up a report, in
the name of the Committee of Legislation, upon
the prisoners of the province of Lecce, endeavouring to prove, in the first place, that real anarchy
reigned in that province in 1817, &c.; in the second,
that it arose from the strife of political parties; and
in the third, that the crimes committed by the prisoners in question were all in consequence of their
various political opinions. He therefore ended by
proposing a decree to suppress all criminal pro-

ceedings against such as had not been tried, and to remit the remainder of the punishment of such as had been already condemned.

The deputy Nicolai, and several of his colleagues, declaimed vehemently against the proposal of the Committee: they observed that, far from extenuating the enormity of crime, the pretence of committing it for the sake of liberty, only served to aggravate it. The majority of votes in the assembly rejected the proposal of the legislative committee, and by their decision, confirmed the general opinion, that the associations of Lecce, in 1817, only used the pretence of politics, to cloak their infamy and rapine.

Accept, Sir, the assurance of the very highest consideration.

&c. &c. &c.

END OF THE MEMOIR

A...G...D...G...M...D...U...

In nome e sotto gli Auspicj dell'A...V... e del nostro Protettore S... Teobaldo

La R...V... sotto il tit... dist... all'Ord... di

A tutte le VV... e BB...CC... regolari sparsi sulla Terra

S... S... S...

Noi G...M... ed Uffiziali della R...V...S... il T...D... regolarmente costituita all'Ord... di

certifichiamo, che il B...C... nativo di

Provincia di di anni di condizione

è membro di questa R...V... al grado Preghiamo tutte le VV... e B...CC... regolari

sparsi sulla Terra di riconoscerlo per tale, e nella della qualità accordargli la considerazione che gli è dovuta e

somministrargli tutti i soccorsi di cui può egli aver bisogno, promettendo di fare noi altrettanto per quelli che c'

interesseranno col nome di B...C...Carbonaro. In fede di che gli abbiamo rilasciato il presente Cert... da noi

sottoscritto, e munito del Bollo, e Sugello di questa R...V... dopo di aver egli apposta la sua firma qui al margine

in nostra presenza

Ord...di li del mese di

Il II° Assist... Il G...M... Il I° Assist...

Il Tesoriere L'Oratore

Il Guarda B...e Sug... Per Mand... della R...V...
Il B...C... Segret...

NE VARIETUR

Patent of an Apprentice

| Filiazione | Statura Capelli Fronte Occhi Naso | | Bocca Mento Carnagione Barba Marche app.te |

A∴ G∴ D∴ G∴ M∴ D∴ U∴

NE VARIETUR

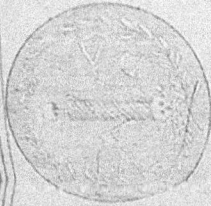

Giustizia — . . . S. . . . . D. .

Morte

N. V. R. M. acon..G. randi

I D D I S L A F. G C I D U G G S

Illustre Gaetano Caffieri i un F.D. Numero 2 unto appartenente alla D.e del S onante tore

quoi sulla superficie della Terra per la sua D.e avuto il piacere di farpaste in questa R. L.D.

Vi dunque invitiamo tutte le f orcità filantropiche a prestarti loro benevole al medesimo ed a soccorerlo

ai suoi bisogni; essendo egli giunto alla D.e di acquistare tu l ttesta di M orte — G gg t:

R. G. M. O. T.

Pietro Gargaro
. . . . .
V.° di Serio 2.° Deoro
Gaetano Caffieri
Registrater di
Morti . . . . .

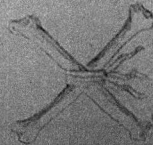

Appendix I

aillet (Vie des Saints, 1er Juillet, 9nie siecle, vers l'an 1017, Paris, 1704,) informs us that St. Thibault or Theobaldus was descended from the first Counts of Brie and Champagne. Surrounded with luxury and riches, his fondness for solitude displayed itself, notwithstanding, at an early age; Thibault refused to marry, or to command the companies which one of his uncles had levied in 1037 against the Emperor Conrad the Salic.[1]

---

1   If St. Theobald was descended from the first Counts of Brie and Champagne, he could scarcely be the nephew of Eudes II. fifth Count of Champagne, who claimed the crown of Burgun-

He quitted his father's house, with a nobleman (Gautier), a friend of his, about 1053; they left their followers and equipage at Rheims, and proceeded on foot into Germany, and in the forest of Piting in Suabia they began to live as poor hermits.

Convinced that they could live only by labour, they occasionally went to the neighbouring villages and hamlets where they worked as journeymen, carrying stones and mortar under the direction of the masons, or laboured in the fields under the reapers, assisted in loading and unloading carriages, cleaned stables with the farmers' servants, and, above all, prepared charcoal for the forges, &c. &c. Notwithstanding their humility, the respect which their virtue gained them in the villages, procured for them honours which they were resolved to avoid by pilgrimage. They returned to France,

---

dy, in opposition to Conrad the Salic, and was killed in battle, 1037, as Eudes himself only succeeded to the title of Count of Champagne and Brie, on the death of Count Stephen without heirs. He might, however, be the nephew of Eudes, if we suppose him the natural son of Theobald, or Thibault, Count of Blois, who was never married, the brother and predecessor of Eudes, in the county of Blois. This line of Blois, Count of Champagne, descended from Thibaut le Tricheur, whose daughter Leutgard married Herbert of Vermandois,[a] of the House of Charlemagne, and first Count of Champagne. This Thibaut was the son of Gerlo, the near relation of Rollo, first Duke of Normandy, and the intermarriage of his posterity with that of Rollo connects them almost equally with the royal race of England. —See Art de Verifier Its Dates. —T.

a   Luitgarde of Vermandois (c. 914 – 978) was the daughter of Herbert II, Count of Vermandois (d. 943) and she married Theobald I of Blois (known as *le Tricheur*—the Trickster) (913 – 975-7). —Ed.

after having walked barefoot to St. Jacques de Compostella in Gallicia. Thibault met his father at Treves in 1054; but that he might not be affected, and so turned from his devotion, he renewed his pious travels with the blessed Gautier. After having adored the tombs of the Apostles at Rome, they went to Venice to embark for the Holy Land, but the war between the Christians and Saracens prevented them from reaching it. In 1056 they set about travelling through various parts of Italy, and after wandering up and down they came to a woody place called Salanigo, near Vicenza, where they established themselves in an old chapel dedicated to the martyrs St. Hermagoras and St. Fortunatus. Gautier died in 1059. Thibault continued in the same place, and lived in the greatest austerity. The Bishop of Vicenza, called Sindeker, raised him to sacred orders, and made him a priest. He obtained from God, even in his life-time, the gift of miracles; but he was tormented by temptations which ceased only two years before his death, at the end of a painful and offensive disease. The fame of his sanctity reached his parents, who went to see him, and his mother established herself in a little cell not far from his own. He expired the last day of June, 1066. Three days before his death there was a considerable earthquake; Thibault's dwelling received five shocks, which were followed by a violent agony, in which he suffered extremely.

There are various opinions as to the place where his remains were deposited; the most authentic account is, that they were carried back from Vicenza to France some years after his death. His relics were distributed in France, Switzerland, and Upper Germany, as far as Vienna in Austria, and in Venice itself, where a parish was founded in his name in 1171, which was called by corruption S. Baldo.

It is said that Thibault was canonised by Pope Alexander III.[2] His principal festival is celebrated in some places on the 30th June, the day of his death; in others, on the 1st July, &c. He is sometimes confounded with St. Thibault de Vengadice, St. Thibault d'Alba, and St. Thibault de Marly de Vaux des Cornay.[3]

---

2   The patron saint of the Carbonari was Theobald of Provins and the latter was canonised by Pope Alexander II. —Ed.

3   The existence of secret religious societies in the reign of Alexander III. has been noticed in the extract from Müller, given in the text. It is remarkable that, about the period of the canonisation of St. Theobald, the patron of the Carbonari, Panvunus placed the foundation of the order of Umilianti by certain Fuorusciti, or banished men of Milan.—See Cronologia Ecclesiastica. —T.

Appendix II

he minutes of the proceedings (at Rome) against the conspiracy of the Carbonari discovered at Macerata have been often mentioned in the preceding Memoir. They contain, in fact, a correct statement of their intentions and mode of proceeding in the Papal states.

These minutes, presented by the Advocate Leggieri, Recorder of the ordinary criminal court of Rome, appointed to conduct this celebrated cause, were printed by order of Government.

The title is—*"A sua Eccellenza reverendissima Monsignor Pacca, Governatore di Roma e Di-*

rettore Generale di Polizia, e sua Congregazione Criminale—Macerata ed altri luoghi di fellonia, contro: Giacomo Papis, il Conte Cesare Gallo, Luigi Carletti, Francesco Riva, il Conte Vicenzo Fattiboni, l'Avvocato Pietro Castellano, Antonio Cottoloni, e Pio Sampaolesi, ed altri, inquisiti, arrestati ed assenti. Ristretto del Processo informativo. Roma, nella Stamperia della Rev. Camera Apostolica."

But as very few copies were printed, it is now become almost impossible to procure one. It has therefore been judged necessary, in order to complete and vivify the picture that has been just drawn, to add an extract from these official notes. The introductory part has been selected in preference, as embracing the whole subject.

"Towards the end of June in the year 1817, a regular proceeding was instituted, by the delegation of Macerata, against certain individuals who were discovered to belong to secret societies, and who had made attempts against the public tranquillity and safety. The active machinations in which the Carbonari of the Papal departments were indefatigably engaged, particularly in the beginning of the autumn of 1816, were directed to the same object. They began to unite more closely, and established Vendite in many places where they had never existed. As they increased in force they sent a confidential agent from Fermo to Bologna, believing that there existed in that city a Supreme Vendita, which regulated all the others. Instead of this they found there the Central Council of the Guelphs, which received the petitions conveyed by the agent, and concerted with him on the means of instituting Guelph Councils. The plan laid down was effected by instituting these councils in places where they had not before existed, as far as the Marches, and composing them of sectaries of all kinds, and particularly of Carbonari.

A secret and impenetrable correspondence was set on foot by them, by means of a dictionary of various words, referable to others of real meaning, with the aid of numbers, and fictitious names, for the safe conveyance of letters to the individuals composing the different councils. The secret societies were united together by a Project which has fallen into the hands of government, and among whose articles there appears a particular engagement—To maintain an extensive and active correspondence among the sectaries, expressly for the communication of the orders of the general centre in Bologna—To augment the number of sectaries, and to obtain monthly information of their progress, and respective qualities; including that of readiness or fitness to bear arms, (*attitudine all' armi,*) as may be gathered from the following articles. Plan of Organization for the Union of Secret Societies, and for establishing an extensive Communication, and an active and secure Correspondence:

1. The Roman state shall be divided, for the present, into three grand divisions; these shall be

divided into primary centers; and these again into secondary centers.

2. The first division in the Legation of Bologna is a primary center; the second division consists of the Legations of Ferrara, Ravenna, and Forli; which last shall be a primary center, as well as Ancona, for the three Marches of Fermo, Macerata, and Ancona, which will form the third division.

6. Every secret society will observe its own constitution, and will act according to its own regulations.

7. In order to have an accurate and active communication, and that the correspondence may be secure, the alphabet of the Guelphs will be adopted.

9. Every representative will attend to the particular interests of the respective society by which he was elected, and will keep up an uninterrupted correspondence with it, in order to secure a free communication with the centers, according to the orders emanating from the general center, (fixed by the same plan at Bologna.)

16. In the monthly statement, particularizing every society subordinate to the primary center, individuals will be classed and described as proprietors, wealthy or otherwise, young, old, titled, fit to bear arms, &c.

In the same plan of organization, it is settled by a particular provision for the Society, that

> Every council that shall have appointed its committee will assign to every individual composing such committee, a certain number of Guelphs,

proportioned to the extent of the society, to instruct them in their duties, and to cultivate a general public feeling.

Those who are at the head of small divisions will be expected to report their own proceedings to the counsellors of those divisions, in order that the latter may acquaint the council with all the advantages resulting from such instructions, and from the influence of the spirit of the Guelphs; that it may reckon upon, and avail itself of, such individuals as are most zealously attached to the great general cause.

Ancona, the center of Guelphism in the Marches, and the principal seat of Carbonarism, went still farther in its zeal, by constituting within its walls the Supreme Vendita, which had been sought in vain at Bologna. Its proceedings were directed to the same object, expressed in the plan already quoted, but it rendered itself singular, by making use of secret passports, consisting of cards of spades and hearts, provided with a dry seal, with the initial letters A. V. A. Alta Vendita di Ancona, in order that the Good Cousins might be recognized without difficulty in their travels, and might receive all those demonstrations of hospitality, which (they say) peculiarly belong to the philanthropic principles of Carbonarism.

This Vendita allotted the distribution of these passports, in the provinces of Romagna and Lombardy, to the sectaries of Bologna, reserving to itself the dispensation of them, in the Marches and the Roman state.

It was expressed in the instructions of these passports, that their system was only known to the First Lights, (the Grand Masters,) in order that "it might be more effectually concealed from the eye of the vigilant wolf; and the necessary signs were added, in case the departure of the Good Cousin should be secret, or that he should be obliged to travel under a *feigned name.*"

In the midst of these insidious proceedings, they did not omit to impose, by means of crime, on the sectaries themselves, as well as on the uninitiated, called by them Pagans, to remove every possible obstacle to the free prosecution of their labours; as well as to confirm the former in the obligations they had contracted, and to convince both of the formidable power of the Society. Several individuals, who were adverse to their maxims, were destined to the poignard, and were actually wounded in a sudden attack, one of them mortally. These victims were, (in addition to their colleague Priola, of S. Elpidio, accused of perjury,) Feliziani, of Ascoli; the advocate Martini, judge in the tribunal at Fermo; the commissary of police Ricci; the legal vicar of Petritoli, D. Ignazio Scarsini; Valeriani, of Montelpare; and the brigadier of Carabiniers, Pastori, who, after repeated threats of death, conveyed in public notices, although he escaped a pistol shot, was afterwards poisoned; &c. such aggressions and homicide (without reckoning that of Pastori) having been committed without any *immediate* cause, in the *night*, by persons *unknown*, and in *disguise.*

In fact, it is a system universally observed by the Carbonari, that every one of them should be armed with a poignard, as the hand grasping a dagger upon the seals of the order denotes; nor do they deny this.

When a new member is admitted to their Society, they brandish these weapons before the novice; intimating that they will be always ready in his defence, if he is faithful to the Society, and that they will shed his blood if he violates his oath.

It is on this account that al the accused, in whatever manner they have confessed, tremble lest they should fall beneath the stilettoes of their colleagues, which would infallibly happen if their confessions were made public. It is on this account they entreat secrecy. The expressions employed by Massone, President of the Supreme Vendita of the Carbonari, and of the Guelph Council at Ancona, on this subject, are very remarkable.

"Giacomo Papis," (this particular mention of his name seems to prove that he is fully informed on this subject) "Giacomo Papis fears the vengeance of the sect much more than the decision of justice in the present cause." This terror, unlike other circumstances of which this is not the place to treat, accounts of itself for the crimes above alluded to. Poison was at last called in to aid the poignard, as fitter to destroy in some circumstances, by placing the assassin in less danger. This atrocious system, notwithstanding the restriction of the chief sectaries, is at this moment followed up by the most abandoned of the order, who are not easily shaken in their resolutions. But their audacity went still farther, although the vigilance of government, towards the end of 1816, was enabled to check the course of these proceedings, by the arrest of some individuals at Ascoli. The sectaries did not desist from the practices above alluded to, but, more insolent then ever, dared to conspire against the sovereign and his throne.

A general revolt, intended to begin in the Marches, and to extend to Bologna, was the object of their earnest and incessant labours. They would have hailed the moment which ended the precious days of the adorable Sovereign Pontiff, (whom God long guard and preserve.)

In fact, it was in the month of April or May of last year, (1817) exactly the period when the recovery of his Holiness was doubtful, that the Supreme Central Council of Bologna committed to Paolo Monti, Grand Master of the Vendita of the Carbonari of Ferrara, a sketch of a plan of revolution, which the latter, by means of the confidential emissary first sent to Bologna, drew up on principles suggested partly by the Central Council, and partly by his own judgment, and that of the other chief sectaries in that province. The period at which this revolution was to take place was, as soon as the chair of St. Peter should be vacant; its extent, all Italy, except Naples; its object, the attainment of liberty and independence: intending, if they failed to obtain it, to place themselves under the protection of a foreign power. This plan was sent to Count Vincenzo Fattiboni, at Cesena, in order that he might communicate it to the Supreme Central Council in Bologna. He returns for answer to Monti, that

> the plan was excellent, and that it was accepted by the Council itself, but that it was necessary to await the decision of the Grand Dignitaries of Milan (the precise expression) upon whom two commissioners (sectaries) had waited to hasten their ratification.

It was also about the same time (27th of March) that the person called Papis sent a letter from Ancona to Count Cesare Gallo, at Macerata, relative to the object of the revolt; it contained the following passage:—"Be active then: for if ever an opportunity was propitious, it is certainly the present, when the just indignation of the people favours our design, and the information we have received assures us of success in our enterprise."

It was also about the same time, that is, between April and May, that the ex-gendarme Francesco Riva, of Forli, one of the principal executive agents, presented at Ancona a plan of a revolt throughout the state, to Papis, who threw it back to him, saying, that he had not sufficient talents to draw up a plan of such importance. Finally, it was at the end of this period, *viz.* May, that Count Gallo proposed to the sectaries of Macerata the execution of the revolt.

In the mean time nothing was left undone which could tend to alienate the attachment of the subjects from the Sovereign, and excite their indignation by ascribing to him (*a lui*) the scarcity of provisions, although occasioned by the inclemency of the preceding seasons. A sonnet was read in a baracca at Ascoli, whose seditious and sacrilegious meaning may be gathered from the following triplet, remembered by one who was present:—

Figli di Bruto, il brando omai scuotete,
Poichè spunta nel ciel, di sangue tinta,
Stella, che batte il rio Tiranno il Prete.[1]

But in the following spring, that of the last year (1817), a secretary in Fermo composed another not less impious, which was circulated among the inferior Vendite.

Sceso dall'Alpi sitibondo il Tauro
Ala Ligure donna il sen trafisse,
L'Aquila avvezza all' Italo tesauro
Sull'Adriatico Lion gli artigli infisse;
L'irsute orecchie avvolte entro il Camauro
Il Lupo Tiberin, che in lacci visse,
Spezzolli, e sete di vendetta, ed'auro,
Quanto ha dal Tebro al Tronto e al Reno afflisse:
Fame intanto di vita i germi adugge,

---

1   Now, Sons of Brutus! lift the blade on high.
     For lo ! emerging from the blood-stained sky.
     The star that blasts the priestly tyranny

Senza che i mostri rei v'abbian riparo,
E pestifero morbo il popol stnigge:
E che più Italia sonnachiosa aspetti?
Perche non string! il preparato acciaro,
E il gran momento del tuo scampo affretti?[2]

During the last winter and spring (1817) fires,
which were reported to have succeeded each other
rapidly, took place, accompanied with the escape
of convicts and prisoners in various places, from
Bologna to Spoleto, where the sectaries particularly abounded. These fires were discovered to be
generally supposititious, although some were really accidental. The escape of prisoners could only
have been effected by co-operation from without.
This, with the support of other arguments, war-

---

2   Fierce from the Alps, the Bull intent on spoil.
    The bosom gores of the Ligurian dame.
    The Eagle, wont to batten on our soil.
    Seeks Adria's Lion with his grasp to tame;
    His shaggy ears in the tiara twin'd.
    The Tyber wolf, who long in thraldom pin'd.
    Bursts from his bonds, and eager to destroy,
    Spreads desolation wide thro' central Italy.[a]
    Famine, the while, checks every germ of life.
    Nor guilty rulers shelter us from ill.
    Death gains the victory that hath no strife:
    Then why, O! slumb'ring Italy, dost wait?
    Where is the sword that thirsts for vengeance still.
    To speed the crisis of thy better fate?

a   The Reno is the main branch of the Po di Primaro, on which Ferrara is built, a few miles South of the Po Grande. The Tronto is a considerable stream in the March of Fermo, which it separates from Abruzzo Ultra, and consequently divides the States of the Church from the kingdom of Naples. —T

ranted the conclusion, that all was owing to the sectaries, whose object was to unsettle the people of those provinces, to promote brigandage, to call the attention of the government forces against robbers, and to divert them from their stations, by which means the intended revolt would have been easily and securely effected.

The sentiments expressed in the letter of Papis, quoted above, were echoed by the speeches of the members in language equally specific, and corresponding with the object of the revolt. Such too were the discourses held by the chief orators and sectaries in various meetings, both before and after the date of Papis's letter. In one of these meetings held at S. Elpidio, the sacred purple was strongly inveighed against, and it was announced that the day would come when it would be changed into a mantle of blood.—*Proc. Mac.* fol. 85. In another, held subsequently in the same place, the necessity of destroying monarchy, and especially the holy authority of the Pope, was set forth; and the sectaries were exhorted to undertake any project, however difficult, for the purpose of regaining liberty.—*Proc. Mac.* fol. 828. 841. 86l. In another, held at S. Ginnesio, it was recommended to the members to provide themselves with arms and ammunition to serve as occasion offered; for, they were told, liberty and independence would soon be attained.—*Proc. Mac.*, fol. 1470, &c. In another, held at Macerata, in inculcating the necessity of rigid attention to secrecy with respect to the operations of the Society, a threat of death by the poignard was expressed against those who should attempt to violate their oath, and it was hinted that the same means would be necessary, ere the happy moment would arrive, when liberty would be regained, and the yoke of the present government thrown off.—*Proc. Mac.*, fol. 218. 296. 690. 979. 1317. &c. At Loreto, on the establishment of the Guelph Council, a discussion was held on the revolution which was shortly to take place, and on the satisfactory accounts of preparations for it, in consequence of which all the sectaries evinced a determination to follow it up.—*Proc. Mac.* 111. &c. At Monte Lupone the same subject was discussed, and the members animated each other to action, declaring themselves eager for the crisis, and exulting in the prospect of establishing an independent republic—*Proc. Mac.*, fol. 137. 201. 220. 236. 283. 467. 594. 605. 704.

Again, at Montolmo, in another assembly, the members were assured that liberty and independence would be soon regained.—*Proc. Mac.*, fol. 781. In another, at Monte Lupone, held on the 5th of June, one of the sectaries, grasping a dagger in his hand, caused his companions to renew their oath of secrecy, and declared that whoever betrayed it should perish by the weapon he held. After this preface he showed the advantages that would be obtained by taking the reins of power out of the hands of the actual government, and by erecting an independent republic. Another member recommended the imitation of Brutus, by dethroning tyrants and destroying monarchy, and by erecting upon their ruins an independent republic—and concluded that in a short time the yoke of the present government would be thrown off, exhorting his associates to provide themselves for this object, even with poisoned weapons (arme anche avvelenate) and with ammunition, in order to be ready on the first opportunity.—*Proc. Mac.*, fol. 100. 105. 114. 124. 138. 140. 155. 160. 180. 201. 209. 211. 222. 224. 239.241. 284. 286. 298. 596. 607. 1559, 1562.

The plan for the execution of the revolt was the most terrible and sanguinary. An incendiary proclamation was to have been circulated in the Marches and other provinces of the state, immediately on the breaking out of the conspiracy in Macerata, to excite the people to join it. To that place the various Vendite of the Carbonari and Councils of the Guelphs, expressly informed of the event, were to have sent, in the same night, a number of armed rebels of their order. These were to have been admitted into the city, in which part of the Sectaries were to have been ready to act. The watchword for the rebel-bands in answer to the challenge, "*Chi evviva?*" was to have been, "*San Teobaldo*" (whom the Carbonari consider the protector of the order.) The other secret word among the leaders was "*Vendetta al Popolo.*" Having insinuated themselves by stratagem into the places where the government troops are stationed, they

would have overpowered them and deprived them
of their arms, confining such as were unwilling to
take a part in their operations. In the same manner, entering the public prisons, they would have
confined the keepers, and released the prisoners,
selecting from the latter those who are fit to bear
arms.

Afterwards dividing the number of the rebels
into patroles of twelve men, some were to have attacked the public treasuries, others the habitations
of rich private individuals whose property was to
have been plundered; and some, known to be hostile to the sect, were to have been seized and conducted to the deep subterraneous cells of the Mon-
astery of Santa Chiara, which was fixed upon as a
rebel station—there they were to be destroyed by
fire or poison, their relations being made to believe
that they were sent as hostages elsewhere. The
plunder, under the faith and responsibility of the
appointed heads of the patroles, was to have been
deposited in the Convent "del Bernabiti," where
others would have registered it, to be afterwards
employed in the necessary expenses. The principal
civil and ecclesiastical authorities would not have
been exempted from seizure and imprisonment.

Four cauldrons of burning pitch, on the sum-
mit of the tower of Macerata, together with sul-
phur rockets let off from the square, would have
announced to the other cities the completion and
success of the revolution.—At sight of this a number of fires, on appointed heights, would have

communicated the result from the Marches to Bologna, in order that the dreadful enterprise and example might have been every where imitated.— The tolling of all the bells on the following morning would have attracted the peasants of the neighbouring country into the city. This was to give the appearance of an insurrection of the people, and to conceal the operations of the sectaries. They would then have proclaimed a free and independent government, and the Conte Cesare Gallo would have been elected Consul with pretended reluctance to assume the office. An inviolable law was to have reduced the most necessary articles of support to a just price.—All taxes were to have been abolished. Public thanksgiving, with the performance of the Ambrosian hymn,[3] was to have been appointed in the Cathedral. A regiment of infantry, and a corps of cavalry were to have been organized with the tempting pay of five pauls a day[4] to each soldier, in order to ensure the immediate consummation of the work.

It appears however that some of the less violent sectaries differed as to the necessity of accompanying the revolution with these horrors. The auspicious improvement and final restoration of the health of the Sovereign Pontiff disconcerted the

---

3   The Ambrosian chant is, or was till very lately, used in the Cathedral service of Milan in honour of its bishop and benefactor, St. Ambrose; the other Latin churches having for many centuries adopted the Gregorin chant. —T.

4   About 2s. 6d. sterling.

seditious intentions of the Central Council, which decided on deferring their execution. But the plot was already too ripe to be laid aside, and the inferior sectaries in the Marches were too deeply involved to free themselves from their engagement or to listen to delay.

The execution of the revolt, after having been already fixed earlier in the month of June, was finally appointed for the night of the 24th of that month, the anniversary of the festival of St. John—and the impious attempt proceeded to its execution by the shortest means. An incendiary proclamation, which had been probably sent from the Marchies to Forli to be printed, had been previously affixed, during the day, in various parts of the former province, and even in Umbria. Its tenor was as follows:

Proclamation

People of the Roman States (*Popoli Pontifici*)! when it is the will of the Most High God to punish nations, he consigns them to the government of idiots.

When He sees that they are sensible of their errors and wills their happiness, he inspires them with courage and commands them to shake off the yoke of oppression (*il barbaro giogo*). People of the Roman States! you have already suffered long enough—the scythe of Pestilence and Famine will complete your destruction and that of our children, if you delay any longer to protect yourselves. To arms, then! to arms! Let your battle-word be the love of your country and compassion (*carità*) for your offspring. To overthrow the despot, to tax the rich and to succour the indigent be your sole objects. You have only to show yourselves resolutely (*col vostro aspetto imponente*) and order and justice will triumph. History already prepares for you a distinguished rank among her heroes. People, to arms! He alone is worthy of life (*viva solo chi*) who loves his country and succours the wretched. The people of the Marches and of Romagna are devoted to our cause. Last evening they embraced it, and are you, blind people, asleep?

* * *

In the night, within and without the city of Macerata, the sectaries mustered in companies, waiting for their associates, who were to join them in greater numbers from the neighbouring towns. Some of these repaired punctually to the appointed places a few miles from the city; but two muskets were incautiously fired near the walls at a sentinel who observed them. The Carabiniers, commanded by Captain Pesci, instantly hastened to the place, as well as to the other points where the rebels were assembled. The latter were disposed to attack, and thus make a beginning of their enterprize, previously to completing it within the walls. They would have done this had the reinforcement of the principal body of the insurgents arrived as had been previously concerted—but the want of these auxiliaries, who did not appear, obliged them to abandon their evil intention and to separate. The principal agents in the plot did not, however, lose sight of their object, but continuing a close correspondence reserved its execution for some fitter opportunity, and in particular that of the vacancy of the Papal throne. With this idea, spreading false political intelligence among themselves which seemed to promise new troubles, new wars and successive changes, they kept alive and stimulated the spirit of sedition.

Meanwhile the police of Macerata lost no time in making the necessary investigation of the events of the night. Some of the criminal agents were arrested and imprisoned during the following days. The necessity, however, of becoming fully acquainted with all their depositions in order to crush future plots, delayed to the end of last November the arrest of the principal delinquents, who were seized about the same time in their respective provinces and conveyed to the castle of St. Angelo and the prisons of the capital.

The trial of all the accused having been at last terminated by means of special Pontifical powers extended to ecclesiastics, the minutes of the investigation, as far as it relates to the projected revolt and the particular offences of those most heavily implicated, (for the other offenders will be treated of separately) are here given. The names of these delinquents are

Giacomo Papis, of Rome, merchant, residing in
Ancona;
Conte Cesare Gallo, di Osimo, residing in Macerata;
Luigi Carleiti, of Macerata, formerly a soldier;
Francesco Riva, of Forli, ex-gendarme;
Cojite Vincenzo Fattiboni, of Cesena; together with
the Advocate
Pietro Castellano, of Ancona, residing in Macerata;
Antonio Cottoloni, of Macerata, and the notary Pio
Sampaolesi, of Ancona.[5]

* * *

The following was the sentence pronounced and
put in execution against them, in the month of October, 1818:—
The Ordinary Criminal Court of the Government Tribunal, composed of

His Eminency Monsignor the Right Reverend Ti-
berio Pacca, Governor of Rome, President;
The Most Illustrious and Right Reverend Signor
Monsignor Marcantonio Olgiati, Clerk of the
Chamber, representing the first Assessor of
Government;
Monsignor Carlo Alessi, second Assessor;
The Signori
Camillo Benzi, first Lieutenant;
Vincenzo Trambusti, second Lieutenant;
Niccola Bruni, exercising the functions of third

---

5   Then follow the minutes of the trial.

Lieutenant, all in quality of Judges.

Francesco Leggieri, Assessor of the General Direction of Police, in the quality of Recorder, under the direction of the Most Illustrious and Right Reverend Signori

Monsignor Belisario Cristaldi, Pro-Attorney-General;

Monsignor Filippo Invernizzi, Attorney for the Poor, (Avvocato dei Poveri), and

Signor Quirino Francini, Chief Notary of the Government Tribunal—

assembled at 24 o'clock of this day in conformity with the intimation published eight days previously, in one of the chambers of the Apostolic Palace of the Government, the usual place, to judge Giacomo Papis, of Rome, &c. Conte Cesare Gallo, &c. &c. accused of felony, together with others under arrest and absent. The proceedings having been opened, and the Divine assistance invoked with the usual prayers: His Eminency Monsignor the Right Reverend the Governor of Rome, President, received from all the members of the court, a declaration that no relationship existed between themselves, nor between them and the accused, within the limits prescribed by the law. Afterwards he directed the chief notary to place upon the table before him the Edict published by the Eminentissimo Pacca, Pro-Secretary of State, the 15th August, 1814, and the other published the 11th August, 1815, by the Most Illustrious and Right Reverend Monsignor Tiberi, then apostolic delegate in Macerata; together with the general proclamations of the government of Rome, and of the Holy Council published under the Pontificate of the sacred memory of Benedict XIV.

The proceedings of the trial having been read, together with the abstract and all the papers respectively for and against the accused; the report of the Recorder (*Relatore*), and the representations and arguments of Monsignor the Pro-Attorney-General, that the punishment decreed should be accordmg to the provisions of the Laws, having been heard: as also the defence derived from printed papers, and *viva voce* by Monsignor the Attorney of the Poor, who moreover declared that he had for this object received the proceedings of the trial and the abstract many days before the intimation to the court. The documents produced in favour of the accused, by Monsignor the Attorney of the Poor, who was the last to speak, and who declared he had nothing more to add, having been read—

The Court—

1. Having found that it is evident from the trial that all the above-named individuals had planned a general revolt, to be executed as occasion offered, in the Pontifical Dominions, making use for this object of the means afforded them by belonging to the sect of the Carbonari, whose aim is the overthrow of legitimate governments—

2. Having found that such a revolt was actually attempted in the night of the 24th of June of last

year, in Macerata, and that according to the plan it would have been accompanied with the murder of good and peaceful citizens and with the plunder and usurpation of private and public property—

3. Having found that the persons called Giacomo Papis and Conte Cesare Gallo held, for the purpose of the revolt, an explicit correspondence which is in the possession of the General Direction of the Police—

4. Having found that the persons named Luigi Carletti, and Francesco Riva, were the most active agents to effect the revolt by the previous circulation of an incendiary proclamation in the Marches, and other parts of the Papal States—

5. Having found that Pietro Castellano was fully acquainted with the correspondence between Papis and Gallo to effect the revolt, and that he himself provoked it by distributing the above seditious proclamation—

6. Having found that Antonio Cottoloni, secretary of the society of Carbonari, in Macerata, who kept the above-mentioned correspondence between Papis and Gallo, as well as other papers relating to the same subject, together with the arms of the latter—

That Pio Sampaolesi, Secretary of the other society of Carbonari, in Ancona, was also fully acquainted with the intended revolt, and had also knowledge of the correspondence between the said society of Ancona and the Central Council of the Guelphs at Bologna—

That Vincenzo Fattiboni, also acquainted with the intended revolt, was the intermediate organ of this correspondence between the said society of Ancona and the Central Council of the Guelphs at Bologna, and that by his means a plan of revolution, to be extended even beyond the Papal Dominions, was presented to the said Central Council—

Has declared, and declares

    Giacomo Papis,
    Conte Cesare Gallo,
    Luigi Carletti,
    Francesco Riva, and
    Pietro Castellano, Guilty; partly by their own confession, and partly convicted of felony, by the whole tenor of the evidence on the trial, and therefore has condemned them to suffer death—

Has declared again, and declares convicted of participation in the same crime,

    Antonio Cottoloni,
    Pio Sampaolesi, and
    Vincenzo Fattiboni; but as they co-operated less directly and efficaciously in the seditious plot, has condemned them to the punishment of the Gallies for life: Has also condemned all the above-named eight individuals to the payment of the expenses of the trial and sentence: has also appointed a day for another court to try the remaining prisoners under arrest and absent:

Has also ordered that the present sentence be communicated, in due form, to the prisoners condemned: Has ordered, finally, that the present sentence be printed, and affixed not only in Rome, but in all parts of the Papal States, to the number of 500 copies.

Done, closed and judged, in Rome, this day and year above-mentioned, all the members of the court having subscribed the original, together with me the undersigned, Chief Notary of the Government Tribunal.

T. PACCA, Governor of Rome and Vice-Chamberlain.
MARC' ANOTNIO OLGIATI, Clerk of the Chamber.
CARLO ALESSI, Assessor.
CAMILLO BENZI, Lieutenant.
VINCENZO TRAMBUSTI, Lieutenant.
NICCOLA BRUNI, Pro-Lieutenant.
FRANCESCO LEGGIERI, Assessor-Recorder.

QUIRINO FRANCINI, Chief Notary.

The above sentence having been reported by me, the undersigned, to his Holiness our Lord Pope Pius VII. happily reigning, his Holiness, by an act of his natural clemency, has determined that the punishment should be lessened and reduced for

Giacomo Papis,
Conte Cesare Gallo,
Luigi Carletti,
Francesco Riva, and

Pietro Castellano, to Perpetual Confinement, under strict custody, in a fortress of State; and for
Antonio Cottoloni,
Pio Sampaolesi, and
Vincenzo Fattiboni, to Confinement for 10 years, under the same custody.

T. PACCA, Governor and Vice-Chamberlain.

A true copy,
QUIRINO FRANCINI, Chief Notary.

The 8th day of October, 1818.

Appendix III

Reception of a Carbonaro

T he *Preparatore* (preparer) leads the *Pagan* (uninitiated) who is to become a member, blindfold, from the closet of reflexion to the door of the Baracca. He knocks irregularly; the *Copritore* (coverer) says to the second assistant, "A Pagan knocks at the door." The second assistant repeats this to the first, who repeats it to the Grand Master; at every communication the Grand Master strikes a blow with an axe.

Grand Master. See who is the rash being, who dares to trouble our sacred labours.

This question having passed through the assistants and *Copritore* to the *Preparatore*, he answers through an opening in the door.

Preparatore. It is a man whom I have found wandering in the forest.

Gr. M. Ask his name, country and profession.

The secretary writes the answer.

Gr. M. Ask him his habitation—his religion.

The secretary notes them.

Gr. M. What is it he seeks among us ?

Prep. Light; and to become a member of our society.

Gr. M. Let him enter.

(The Pagan is led into the middle of the assembly; and his answers are compared with what the Secretary had noted.)

Gr. M. Mortal, the first qualities which we require, are frankness, and contempt of danger. Do you feel that you are capable of practising them?

After the answer, the Grand Master questions the candidate on morality and benevolence; and he is asked, if he has any effects, and wishes to dispose of them, being at the moment in danger of death; after being satisfied of his conduct, the Grand Master continues, "Well, we will expose you to trials that have some meaning—let him make the first journey." He is led out of the Baracca—he is made to journey through the forest—he hears the rustling of leaves—he is then led back to the door, as at his first entrance.

Gr. M. What have you remarked during this first journey?

(The Pagan relates accordingly.)

Gr. M. The first journey is the symbol of human virtue: the rustling of leaves, and the obstacles you have met in the road, indicate to you, that weak as we are, and struggling in this vale of tears, we can only attain virtue by good works, and under the guidance of reason, &c. &c. Let him make the second journey.

(The Pagan is led away, and is made to pass through fire; he is made acquainted with the chastisement of perjury; and, if there is an opportunity, he is shown a head severed from the body, &c. &c. He is again conducted into the Baracca.)

Gr. M. The fire through which you have passed is the symbol of that flame of charity, which should be always kindled in our hearts, to efface the stains of the seven capital sins, &c. &c.

Make him approach the sacred throne, &c.

Gr. M. You must take an irrevocable oath; it offends neither religion nor the state, nor the rights of individuals; but forget not, that its violation is punished with death.

The Pagan declares that he will submit to it; the Master of the Ceremonies leads him to the throne, and makes him kneel on the white cloth.

Gr. M. Order!

The Oath

I, N. N. promise and swear, upon the general statutes of the order, and upon this steel, the avenging instrument of the perjured, scrupulously to keep the secret of Carbonarism; and neither to write, engrave, or paint any thing concerning it, without having obtained a written permission. I swear to help my Good Cousins in case of need, as much as in me lies, and not to attempt any thing against the honour of their families. I consent, and wish, if I perjure myself, that my body may be cut in pieces, then burnt, and my ashes scattered to the wind, in order that my name may be held up to the execration of the Good Cousins throughout the earth. So help me God.

Gr. M. Lead him into the middle of the ranks (this is done). What do you wish? The Master of the Ceremonies suggests to the Pagan, to say *Light.*

Gr. M. It will be granted to you by the blows of my axe.

The Grand Master strikes with the axe—this action is repeated by all the apprentices—the bandage is removed from the eyes of the Pagan—the Grand Master and the Good Cousins hold their axes raised.

Gr. M. These axes will surely put you to death, if you become perjured. On the other hand, they will all strike in your defence, when you need them, and if you remain faithful. (To the Master of the Ceremonies,) Bring him near the throne, and make him kneel.

Gr. M. Repeat your oath to me, and swear to observe exactly the private institutions of this respectable Vendita.

The Candidate. I ratify it and swear.

Gr. M. Holding the specimen of wood in his left hand, and suspending the axe over the head of the candidate with his right, says. To the great and divine Grand Master of the universe, and to St. Theobald, our protector—In the name and under the auspices of the Supreme Vendita of Naples, and in virtue of the power which has been conferred upon me in this respectable Vendita, I make, name and create you an apprentice Carbonaro.

The Grand Master strikes the specimen which is held over the Apprentice's head, thrice; he then causes him to rise, and instructs him in the sacred words and touch.

Gr. M. Master of the Ceremonies, let him be acknowledged by the apprentices.

The Assistants anticipate the execution of this order, by saying to the Grand Master, All is according to rule, just and perfect.

Gr. M. Assistants, tell the respective orders to acknowledge, henceforth, the Good Cousin N. N. as an active member of this Vendita, &c. &c.

The Symbolical Picture is explained to the new apprentice.

Gr. M. At what hour do the Carbonari terminate their sacred labours?

First Assistant. As soon as the Sun no longer enlightens our forest.

Gr. M. What hour is it?

Second Assistant. The Sun no longer enlightens our forest.

Gr. M. Good Cousins, as the Sun no longer enlightens our forest, it is my intention to terminate our sacred labours. First, let us make a triple salutation (*Vantaggio*), to our Grand Master, divine and human, (Jesus Christ).—To St. Theobald, our protector, who has assisted us and preserved us from the eyes of the pagans—Order! To me,———&c. The signs and salutations (*Vantaggi*) are performed.

Gr. M. I declare the labours ended; retire to your Baracche—retire in peace.

* * *

Reception to the Second Rank

The signs of the Masters are made, and they arrange themselves in order. The Grand Master on this occasion is called the President—The assistants. Counsellors of the College of R. (Respectable) Carbonarism.

The President. At what hour do the Counsellors meet?

First Counsellor. When the cock crows.

President. Second Counsellor, what hour is it?

Second Counsellor. Noon by the sun.

The Counsellors make the triple salutation to the Grand Master, divine and human, and to St. Theobald, and invoke their blessing on their labours. The President puts on a robe, and takes the name of Pilate; the First Counsellor that of Caiaphas;

the second that of Herod; the Adept (*Esperto*) calls himself the chief of the guards; the Master of the Ceremonies, the Godfather; the Good Cousins generally are called the *People*.

The Godfather blinds the eyes of the novice, and makes him journey through the forest; he afterwards leads him towards the President, who causes his crown of thorns, and specimen, to be brought, and questions him on the catechism of the apprentices.

The President. Good Cousin, your trials as anovice are not sufficient to raise you to an equality with us; you must undergo more important trials; reflect upon it, and tell us your intention.

The Apprentice declares that he is ready to undergo the trials.

President. Conduct him to the Olives.

He is led to the place so called—he is placed in a supplicating attitude, his hands lifted towards heaven—the Godfather causes him to repeat aloud:

If the pains I am about to suffer can be useful to mankind, I do not ask to be delivered from them. Thy will be done, and not mine.

Pilat. Let him drain the cup of bitterness.

He is made to drink, and he is then led bound to Pilate.

Pilat. Who is this you bring me ?

Chief of the Guards. One accused of sedition; we found him in the midst of wretches who listened to him, and who are witnesses of his wicked precepts.

The People. He is a seducer of the people, who, to govern despotically, and to overthrow our religion, calls himself the living God.

Pilat. The crime is heavy; I cannot judge him alone. Take him to Caiaphas.

The Chief of the Guards accompanies him.

Chief of the Guards, Pilate sends you this man, to judge him according to his crimes.

Caiap. From what I have heard, he is guilty; his punishment belongs to the Sovereign, Lead him to Herod.

Herod. Who art thou?

The Godfather instructs the novice to say, I am the Son of God.

The People. You hear him, he blasphemes, and deserves the severest punishment.

Herod. Is it true that thou art the Son of the living God?

The Godfather instructs the novice to say.

Thou sayest it.

Herod. People! This is a man who is beside himself; put a white robe upon him, and lead him to Pilate, to judge the man as he thinks fit. The tunic is put upon the novice, he is led to Pilate who shows him to the people.

Pilat. The Prince sends me this man; what will you that I shall do to him ?

The People. Condemn him.

Pilat. I will not condemn him without having heard him. Who are you?

The Godfather for the novice—Jesus of Nazareth, King of the Jews.

Pilat. If he is a king, let a crown of thorns be put upon his head, and a sceptre in his hand: (turning towards the people) Are you satisfied ?

The People. No; he deserves a greater punishment.

Pilat. Strip him, bind him to this column, and scourge him.

Pilate causes him to be again clothed, in a red robe; shows him to the people, and says,

Pilat. Are you satisfied? Behold the man.

The People. No, let him be crucified.

Pilat. I have done my duty; you wish his death; I give him up to you; I wash my hands of the deed; the innocent blood be upon you and on your children. [After Pilate has washed his hands, the novice is delivered over to the people, who make him carry his cross to Calvary; his pardon is asked; he is made to kneel upon the white cloth; the President takes off the red robe, and says,

President. Do you consent to take your second oath? [If he consents, the bandage is taken from his eyes; he is made to kneel on his left knee, with his right hand on the axe. All the Good Cousins arrange themselves in order.

Form of the Oath

I, N. N. promise and swear before the Grand Master of the universe, upon my word of honour, and upon this steel, the avenging instrument of the perjured, to keep scrupulously and inviolably the secrets of Carbonarism; never to talk of those of the Apprentices before the Pagans, nor of those of the Masters before the Apprentices. As also, not to initiate any person, nor to establish a Vendita, without permission, and in a just and perfect number—not to write or engrave the secrets—to help even with my blood, if necessary, the Good Cousins Carbonari, and to attempt nothing against the honour of their families. I consent, if I perjure myself, to have my body Cut in pieces, then burnt, and the ashes scattered to the wind, that my name may remain in execration with all the Good Cousins Carbonari spread over the face of the earth. So help me God.[1]

Some other ceremonies follow—the new Master is instructed in all the signs of his rank, &.c. &c. The close of the proceedings is the same as that of the apprentices:

---

1   We learn from the minutes of the Roman trial that the Republican Brother Protectors swear, over a phial of poison, or a red hot iron, "never to divulge the secrets of the Society; to labour day and night for the extirpation of tyrants." They submit, in case of perjury, to the punishment of dying by poison, and having their flesh burnt by the red hot iron.

1st Rank	Pass-Word	Sacred Words	Touch
			C _____ .. These Signs and Touches are made with the middle finger on the right thumb of the Fellow-Apprentice.

Decorations of the Apprentice

Three ribbons—black, blue and red, with the specimen of wood.

2nd Rank	Pass-Word	Sacred Words	Touch
			O _____ .. The Signs and Touches are made with the middle finger of the right thumb of the Fellow-Master.

Decorations of the Master

The specimen of silver, with a tricoloured scarf—black, blue and red.

*Regulations and Privileges of the Supreme
Lodge or Alta Vendita at Naples.*

Section II.

Of the Statutes of the Order of Carbonarism

Art. 1. The Supreme Vendita is composed of honorary members and deputies of each particular Vendita.

Art. 2. This body is legislative and executive at the same time: it combines in itself all powers, and is appointed unalterably at Naples.

Art. 3. It is the province of the Supreme Vendita alone to establish dependent Vendite, and to grant them constitutions emanating from the Supreme Vendita itself, or furnished with its *Seen and Approved.*

Art. 4. The Supreme Vendita only recognizes as Grand Masters or representatives of Vendite those who have been elected by the free vote of such Vendite.

Section III.

Art. 1. The direction of the proceedings in the Supreme Vendita is confined to officers named by its members.

Art. 2. The officers consist of seven grand dignitaries and others lower in rank.

Art. 3. The grand dignitaries are: one Grand

Master, two Adjutants, one Grand Administrator General, two Grand Conservators General, and one Grand Representative of the Grand Master.

Art. 4. The offices of these dignitaries are triennial.

Art. 5. The Honorary Officers are as follow: one Ordinary Representative of the Grand Master, one Grand Conservator, one First and one Second Assistant, one Grand Orator, one Grand Treasurer,[2] one Grand Keeper of the Seals, one Grand Keeper of the Archives, two Grand Masters of the Ceremonies, one Grand Almoner, two Grand Master Adepts (*Esperti*) and two Grand Adepts (*Esperti*.)

Art. 6. The offices of the Honorary Officers are triennial.

Art. 7. The Ordinary Officers are: three Presidents, three First and three Second Assistants, three Orators, three Secretaries, one Treasurer, three Keepers of the Seals, three Keepers of the Archives, one Assistant Treasurer, four Masters of the Ceremonies, one Almoner, one Accountant, eight Adepts (*Esperti*.)

Art. 8. The exercise of their functions is triennial; but they can be re-elected.

Art. 9. The number of active officers is thirty-one; it will be increased in proportion to the increase of the Good Cousins Carbonari.

---

2   The Good Cousins pay a regular contribution; they are taxed according to the wants of the Society: the funds for charity are collected by questors.

SECTION IV.

Art. 1. The Supreme Vendita has, besides its general assemblies, three private divisions; that is to say, one Grand Vendita of Administration, one of Legislation, and a third of Counsel and Appeal.

On the day of St. Theobald all those in office or who are in any way responsible must give an account of the discharge of their duties.

Appendix IV

Edict

HERCULES, Deacon of S. Agata alia Suburra, Cardinal Consalvi, Secretary of State to His Holiness Our Lord Pope Pius VII.

If from the period of the ancient Roman Legislation severe penal prohibitions have been issued against secret and hidden Associations, whose clandestine proceedings were sufficient to give room for supposing either that some seditious conspiracy against the state and the public tranquillity was plotted, or that a school for depravity existed in them; with much more reason have the Sovereign Pontiffs been justified in looking in the same light upon the Associations known under the names of Free-Masons, Illuminati, Egiziani, and such like. And as they accompany their works of darkness with forms, ceremonies, rites, oaths of secrecy, suspected at least, and especially with the indiscriminate admission of persons of all classes and nations and of whatever conduct or religion: it is impossible not to entertain a just suspicion that they aim not only at the subversion of thrones but also of Religion, and especially of the true and only one of Jesus Christ, of which the Roman Pontiff was, by its divine Founder and Legislator, constituted the Head, the Master and the Guardia.

Influenced by these reasons and animated by their zeal, although they did not witness the ruinous development (too plainly apparent in our own time) of these secret and infernal societies: the Popes Clement XII. and Benedict XIV. of glorious memory, resisted, with all the vigour of their Apostolic Office, the already threatening disorder. The first, with his decree beginning "*In eminenti Apostolatus specula,*" published 27th April, 1738, not only prohibited and condemned altogether the assemblies and meetings of the said Free-Masons, or such like, whatever denomination they might assume, but also passed on the individuals enlisted and initiated in the same, in whatever rank, and on their advisers and abettors, the sentence of excommunication, to be incurred *ipso facto*, without need of any information, and for which absolution could only be given by the Roman Pontiff *pro tempore*, except in case of death. His immediate successor Benedict XIV., perceiving the high importance and necessity of this measure, especially for the good of the Catholic Religion and for the public safety, in another decree beginning *"Providas Romanorum Pontificum"* published 18th May, 1751, not only fully confirmed that of his predecessor, inserting it in his own, word for word, but moreover with his usual wisdom stated in detail the weighty reasons which ought to induce every government in the world to join in the same prohibition, which public experience had rendered almost superfluous to repeat even to the simplest of people. Nor did their care and foresight stop here. The mere horror of crime and the thunders of the Ecclesiastical censures, which are sufficient to warn and shake the conscience of the good, have generally little effect on the depraved accompanied by the apprehension of external suffering. On this account the Pope Clement XII., by means of an Edict published by Cardinal Giuseppe Firrao, his secretary of state, dated 14th January, 1739, pronounced the severest temporal punishments against the offenders, and at the same time took measures to ensure the execution of the order; and the sacred memory of Benedict XIV., in the act above quoted, to give authority to these measures, recommended to the magistrates all possible vigilance and energy in their execution.

But in the general confusion which has taken place during past events, as well in the state as in the Church, these just, salutary and indispensable provisions have been contemned with impunity, and the Societies and Assemblies above mentioned, found every facility not only of establishing themselves in Rome, but of spreading themselves over various parts of the States His Holiness our Lord Pope Pius VII., anxious therefore to remedy without delay an evil which requires a speedy and determined check, lest it insinuate itself like a canker to infect the whole body of the state, commands and directs us to make known to all, his sovereign determinations, which shall, in virtue of the present Edict, have the full force of laws, and shall serve to regulate the tribunals and the judges in both courts, as well as in all cities, towns, lands, and provinces belonging to the temporal dominion of the Apostolic throne.

That is to say, that, with respect to the court of conscience and the ecclesiastical penalties which may be incurred by unfortunate persons, who, in time past or to come (which God forbid, especially for his Holiness beloved subjects) may have the misfortune to take a part in any way whatever in the said criminal Masonic societies and assemblies. His Holiness subjects them in all respects to the provisions and penalties expressed in the above acts of his glorious predecessors, which he hereby renews and confirms (if necessary) in all their force. Influenced therefore by the most lively feelings of his pastoral zeal, and of his paternal heart, the Holy Father reminds and earnestly recommends all and each of the faithful who find themselves so misled, as they value their eternal welfare, seriously to think and reflect into what an abyss of perdition they have plunged their souls, oppressed by such an enormous transgression, and by the excommunication which excludes them from every benefit of the ecclesiastical communion, and must accompany them to that tremendous tribunal, where nothing is concealed, and where all the aids and interests of the world disappear. Let them therefore return by means of a sincere penitence to the arms of the Church, their compassionate mother, who invites them, and is ready to receive them affectionately, and to effect their reconciliation with the Great Father of Mercy, whom they have ungratefully forsaken.

With respect to the civil court. His Holiness is willing to extend his sovereign clemency here also, as far as is compatible with the police regulations of a well conducted state, as to what might have occurred during the unfortunate times of disorder and impiety which have preceded his happy return, and the publication of the present Edict. Before those times this deadly pestilence had scarcely, if at all, infected the territory and subjects of the Pope. Many however have suffered themselves to be seduced by circumstances; and as the Holy

Father deplores the fatal error of these men, so he would wish to be able for ever to forget it—but it is for them to merit such clemency by a speedy and lasting repentance, at least in their external conduct, for which every citizen is responsible to society. For the present, therefore, it is sufficient for them to know and to bear in mind that the government is acquainted with them, that it knows the precise places where they were accustomed to meet, that a strict watch will be kept upon them, and that the names of their principal agents will be communicated to the Presidents of the courts, in order to prevent any recurrence of the offence. And in any case of such recurrence, past transgressions will be brought forward in aggravation. No person can henceforth protect himself with the old pretext that he did not see any harm in that preparatory course of actions sometimes indifferent and ridiculous, by which the initiated were artfully amused, in order to be afterwards employed in the mysteries of this wicked system. In order, therefore, to establish just and necessary precautions for the future:—

It is forbidden, in conformity with the dispositions of the above mentioned Edict of the 14th January, 1739, in the first place, to any person whatever, as well in Rome as in the whole Papal dominions, to continue, renew, re-establish, or institute assemblies of those persons called Free-Masons, or other similar assemblies of whatsoever denomination, ancient or modern, or recently invented under the name of Carbonari, which last have circulated a pretended Pontifical Brief of approbation, which bears on its face the evidence of falsehood and fabrication. It is forbidden to be enrolled, or to be present in any of these societies, even for once, under whatever colour or pretext, or to seek for, instigate, or tempt any one to join them, or to afford knowingly the accommodation of a house or any other place for their meetings, either for rent, as a loan, or according to any contract whatever, or to afford them aid, counsel, or protection, in any way whatever.

This prohibition shall also extend to those subjects who shall infringe the order by any relation direct or indirect, mediate or immediate, with such societies erected, or to be erected, without the Papal States.

It shall not be lawful for any person to keep in his possession or elsewhere, instruments, arms, emblems, statutes, memorials, patents, or any thing whatever, relating to the proceedings of the said societies.

Whoever shall receive intimation that such secret and clandestine meetings are still held, or shall be invited to attend, enter, or be enlisted therein, shall instantly inform the governor of Rome (as far as regards the capital) or the heads of provinces, and Apostolic delegates. And those who, in obedience to the present article, shall be obliged to give information, are assured that that information shall be inviolably kept secret, that they shall even be sometimes pardoned the penalty they may have incurred by belonging to, or having been an accomplice of, such societies, and that they shall receive a proportionate pecuniary reward, at the charge of the offenders, on presenting the usual proofs, sufficient to verify their accusation; and on this subject His Holiness expressly orders that all be made aware, that in this natural and Christian obligation to reveal a wicked conspiracy to those that can prevent consequences threatening the order of the commonwealth and of religion, there can be no dishonour nor impropriety; and that whatever oath to the contrary may have been taken, it would become a bond of iniquity, which all know imposes no obligation to maintain it, and which leaves the contrary duty free.

The penalties for those who transgress the above regulations shall be severe corporal punishment, proportioned to the nature, fraud (*dolo*), and circumstances of the offence, and to which will also be added partial or total confiscation of possessions and pecuniary fines, which the ministers and officers of justice shall also share, in proportion as they shall have usefully and effectually exerted themselves for the discovery, trial, and punishment of the delinquents, according to justice. His Holiness especially wills and orders that the buildings, whatever they may be, as Palaces, Houses, Villas, or other places, however walled or enclosed, in which the said societies meet or hold their Lodges, as they are called, shall, as soon as the special proofs shall appear on trial, be immediately confiscated, reserving for the proprietor of the ground, if ignorant and innocent of the proceeding, the right of indemnification at the cost of the offenders. Finally, all presidents of courts and officers of justice are directed carefully and diligently to see to the execution of the present dispositions, it being understood, that whatever doubt may arise, they are to address themselves, without delay, to the office of the Secretary of State, to have the supreme decision of His Holiness.

Dated at the Secretary of State's Office, the 15th August, 1814.

B. Card. Pacca, Chamberlain of the Holy Church, and Pro-Secretary of State.

Appendix V

Remonstrance of the Society of the Carbonari to the Sovereign Pontiff Pius VII

O Blessed Father,

I f it behoves every man to preserve his own honour uninjured, and to keep his own reputation unspotted, how much more jealous of these ought any Society to be, living in the state; especially where the religion of the country is the same as that which the Society professes. It is this sentiment so worthy of citizens professing the Catholic and Apostolic religion of our Lord Jesus Christ that animates the Society of the Carbonari to appeal to your Holiness with that humble respect which is due to the Vicar of Him who was God and man, in order to prepare your Holiness to receive the petitions and to understand the feelings of the Society—that, when it is found to be irreproachable in religion and morals, and that it conforms to the laws of the Gospel, your Holiness may be disposed to alter the opinion you once conceived of it, as well as the decrees which your Holiness thought proper to issue against it in your Bull of the year 1815. This will not be the first time that the visible Head of the Church, undeceived by evidence, has revoked Bulls and Decrees. The example of your predecessors will be imitated by your Holiness in circumstances of much greater importance than the quarrels of monasteries and the scholastic disputes of friars, on which subjects justice often thought fit to recall decrees which had been the result of an ignorance of facts. Let your Holiness deign then, with your superior intelligence, to examine the petitions of this Society, and weigh their arguments with that spirit which does not belong to human policy, but which is worthy of the Vicar of Christ, whose kingdom is not that of the world. It appears that the fears and suspicions of the Popes have been excited by the formation of Societies, which, separating themselves from the rest of the people, have adopted a secret discipline. The vigilance of the head of the Church, suspecting that the secret might contain sentiments contrary to the true religion, and the sound morality of the Gospel, has threatened to employ its thunders to separate from the communion of the Faithful those who endanger its unity. Hence the Bulls of the former Pontiffs, and above all, that of your Holiness, which is particularly aimed at this Society of the Carbonari, who are now at your feet to remove from the mind of your Holiness the suspicions which induced you to take that step. Polished nations, from the remotest antiquity, have had their Secret Societies, either Philosophical or Sacerdotal. Philosophy, knowing the vulgar to be incapable of understanding theoretical truths, which, if made public, instead of instructing, would have involved men of no education in scepticism, endeavoured to spread over certain physical and moral truths a veil through which it was given to the learned alone to penetrate. The priesthood adopted its fables, in order that, while the people were satisfied with these and with the outward apparatus of Mythology, the Sacerdotal Societies might keep to themselves the sacred science for which the vulgar have been ever unfit. The History of Egypt, that of the Assyrians, of the Schools of Philosophy, in Greece, the Traditions of Cosmogony, the Systems of Mystic Regenerations, the Sacred Colleges of the Syrites, are all so many proofs of these truths—while the fate of Socrates, the greatest philosopher of antiquity, who did not sufficiently conceal from the vulgar the secret of his school, was the means of rendering the discipline of the Sacerdotal as well as Philosophical Societies even still more impenetrable from that period.

But in the mean time, why did not the Sovereigns take any umbrage at these societies? It can only be accounted for by supposing that they were fully instructed in this secret discipline; and hence, knowing it to be in conformity with good order, and analogous to social happiness, notwithstanding the vain attempts of ignorant and impatient curiosity, they deigned to afford them protection.—Was not the Church itself, of Jesus Christ, from its origin to the period of the Victory of Constantine over the tyrant Maxentius, a secret Society? Was not its discipline concealed? What monstrous ideas against the Society did not the concealment of its mysteries and sacred rites excite, not less in the minds of the Sovereigns than of the Pagans generally? A glance at the works of our Apologists shows us that the secret so jealously kept by our fathers was the means of their being looked upon as infanticides, as adorers of beasts, as magicians, and as sworn enemies to the State, notwithstanding the sanctity of those who belonged to the society, and in spite of their good conduct and of that spirit of charity which taught them not only to obey, but even to offer up their most fervent prayers to God for the happiness of a state in which their life was daily sought. Constantine himself entertained such an idea of the Christian society till, he was acquainted with its true and genuine object—so that, although from being a fresh convert he could not penetrate to the knowledge of the mysteries, as soon as he found that the secret kept by the society was not only not opposed to the happiness of the state, but formed its most solid support, he immediately de-

clared the Christian church a legitimate body, protecting it against the efforts and most earnest petitions not of the vulgar alone, but of the powerful
class of Pagan Priests. The Society of the Carbonari
does not doubt, therefore, that as soon as the secret discipline it preserves (and which ought not to
be suspected because it is secret, but only because
it may be contrary to the profession of the Catholic religion) is made manifest—the knowledge of
its purity and adherence to the Gospel, and to the
most holy laws of the Church, will secure it from
the prejudices which the vulgar entertain against
it, as well as from the threat which your Holiness
thought fit to publish in your last Bull.

The Roman Catholic and Apostolic Religion,
that which our fathers have ever maintained un-
impaired (*intemerata*), that which acknowledges
in your Holiness the Vicar of Him who was God
and man, who, with his Divine blood, founded the
sublime, true, and only religion, this is the only
one which in the spirit of truth is preserved and
professed by the Society of the Carbonari.

Every Society has its liturgy. That of the Carbonari breathes only the religion of Jesus Christ.
The cross, the sign of our religion, forms a principal part of its rites—Faith, Hope, Charity, devices
of the Catholic church, according to the Apostle St.
Paul, form the language which distinguishes the
Society, and by means of which it communicates.
The conduct which is inculcated in the education
of the Carbonari is precisely the practice of the

morality of the Gospel. The most eminent among the precepts of this divine morality, that of universal charity, not only binds them together, but obliges them to practise it, even towards those who do not belong to the Society. It is true that such a society has a political object; but this is not in the slightest degree contrary to the maxims of religion. It preserves that respect to sovereignty which the Apostle requires from Christians—it loves the Sovereign, it preserves the State, and even the succession of families; but it supports a democracy, which, instead of offending monarchy, forms that happy addition to it which endears it more to the nation, and which alone can render the rights of empire and those of the citizen less fluctuating, and which, therefore, prevents political disorders by constitutional means, and consolidates the true basis of national felicity, a felicity to which the Christian religion directly leads those nations that have the glory to profess it.

Such, most blessed Father, is the state, the object, and the secret of the Society of the Carbonari. Far from that secret, now no longer such, be every suspicion as to its dogmas or morals. If it separate itself from the public, if it hold its meetings apart, if it have its peculiar rites, it is answered that all this is necessary to preserve the spirit that distinguishes it. Man is, in a manner, subject to the senses.—Truth veiled in rites, which are its symbols, insinuates itself more firmly into the mind; and a ceremony which inspires the newly initiated with a sacred horror, is warranted even by that once imposed upon the proselytes of the church.

The rite which is still preserved in the administration of baptism, is respected because it is figurative, although it does not correspond with the actual state of the infant christian. But the ceremonies of the Society of the Carbonari are in no wise opposed to the profession of the Catholic and Apostolic Religion, which its members jealously maintain.

It is also true that, as in the most religious Society, so also in that of the Carbonari, there may be persons whose manners and conduct do not correspond with the fundamental principles of the Society, nor with its regular discipline. But it is a truth generally admitted, that we should never argue on the object of a body from the acts of its members, as it would then be difficult to oppose any one who might be disposed to judge of the sanctity of our own religion from the actions of any particular minister of the altar. If your Holiness wishes to judge of this Society, if you wish to be assured of the uniformity of its principles and its conduct, deign to look upon what has taken place in this kingdom in the two last months. This Society, preserving, in word and deed, a profound respect for religion, and exhibiting with splendour, but without ostentation, a morality worthy of the first ages of the church, has conducted to perfection the greatest and most important of civil and political operations, with a degree of order, tranquillity, and success, unexampled in the history of past ages—letting Europe know by what new mode a Society, well fixed in the sound principles of the religion of Christ, and in the practice of the morality of the Gospel, has been enabled to raise upon the wings of peace (*sulle ali della pace*), a work, which has elsewhere cost so much blood to the stranger and to the citizen.

The Society of the Carbonari, therefore professing, the dictates of the church of Jesus Christ, the Roman Catholic and Apostolic Religion, whose visible head it acknowledges in your Holiness—practising a moral discipline entirely modelled on that of the Gospel—no longer having a secret which leaves room for suspicion, now that it has revealed its great object, and that the Sovereign, like the real Father of the nation, has adopted it with sincerity (*conpienezza di cuore*), employing a ceremonial whose symbols are only figurative of that which has been executed with so much applause; your Holiness neither has, nor can have reason to suspect this Society, either as to religion or morals; on which account it is time, now that your mind is undeceived, and freed from those suspicions which provoked against the Society the thunders of the Vatican, that you cease to class it among equivocal secret societies, rendered public and general as it is in this kingdom under the auspices of our most religious Sovereign, and of his most pious Vicar-General the Hereditary Prince Francis, and consequently that you declare it free from the spiritual penalties which you pronounced against it with your Bull of the year 1815, when neither its dispositions, professions nor object were known.—Such a declaration, which the simple truth, unaided by the illusions of elaborate eloquence, demands, at the same time that it will give additional lustre to the spirit of Evangelical docility which characterizes the Sovereign Pontiff, who, walking in the steps of the Apostles, rather than support with worldly policy a decree which was the offspring of ignorance as to facts, knows how to recall it in time, will also restore peace to those consciences that, divided by doubts, are prevented from partaking in the acts of religion to which they are attached. Considerations, which must immediately interest the feelings of the Pontiff (Santa Sede) and which will secure the public tranquillity of the State, so that every avenue may be shut against the ill-intentioned, and the perfidious enemies of national happiness, and in this Society may the Holy See (Santa Sede) at all times meet with respect, obedience, docility, and the most lasting and humble gratitude.

Naples, 9th September, 1820.

Appendix VI

The following document is translated as literally as possible, some lines of introduction only are suppressed, and some inflated phrases, as well as the eternal epithets of valiant, excellent, &c. &c. with which every name is loaded in the original.

Historical Statement of the Facts which Preceded and Produced the Movement of the Second Battalion of Nola.

Et quorum pars magna fui.—Virg.

et the friends of their country deign to read a rapid statement of operations which are perhaps worthy of a tribute of love. The Good Cousin Francesco Maria Gagliardi, of the Province of Salerno, so far back as the month of May, 1817, had conceived the plan of a revolution. He conferred to this effect with the Good Cousins Domenico and Gabriele Abatemarco, brothers and his countrymen, and with the Good Cousin Michele de Blasiis, of Basilicata. The Good Cousin Ferdinando Arcovito, who now presides at one of the Government Courts of Justice, joined them and promised them the co-operation of the brave General Arcovito, his relation. It was resolved to despatch Gagliardi to Calabria, to the G. C. Rinaldi, a Carmelite, possesses great influence in that province. A plan was formed, and the establishment of a Central Committee of correspondence was attempted at Naples. To accomplish this, the GG. CC. Gagliardi and Abatemarco contrived an interview with the G. C. Rosario Macchiaroli, then President of the Supreme Magistracy of the Carbonari of Salerno. This interview took place at Pompeii, in the presence of some other GG. CC. from Naples and Salerno. It was not till after this time Gagliardi proceeded to Calabria, to confer with Rinaldi, while the brothers Abatemarco sent circulars from Naples in order to be in correspondence with several points. Gagliardi returned, and it was thought proper to defer the enterprize, it being found that the province of Principato Citra[1] alone was well organized, and that it was necessary to wait till the others were equally so. Let it be permitted to us here to pay a just tribute of gratitude to this noble province, which, under the direction of the brave Macchiaroli, invited that of Basilicata and Avellino to follow its glorious example.

---

1   Under the name of the Lucullian Republic.

In the mean time all the GG. CC. hereafter named, never ceased their exertions, and despised the dangers with which they were menaced by an active and vigilant police. But after three years of constant care, the force of the Carbonari had become formidable, a great portion of the troops had joined this liberal order; several provinces were organized and united by correspondence with the Supreme Magistracy of Salerno, &c.

In the month of March of the present year, the example of Spain raised enthusiasm to its height. Gagliardi was at Naples, and lived with Gherardo Curci, of Basilicata. Both perceived that the epoch of the regeneration of their country was arrived. The first project they formed, was that of revolutionizing the troops, when they should be encamped in the plains of Sessa. This plan was communicated to the G. C. Vincenzo Bologna, lieutenant of dragoons, an officer distinguished by his patriotic zeal. He consented and promised to range his whole regiment, which had already received orders to prepare to march to the camp, under the sacred standard of liberty. A meeting took place between Gagliardi, Curci, Bologna, the brothers Raffaello, and Tommaso Marrello, Scarpa of Principato Citra, the brothers Michele, and Gennaro de Blasiis, and the brothers Abatemarco; and the operations were arranged, which were to be carried into effect at the camp, on the arrival of the dragoons; but this plan did not take effect because of a counter-order, which kept the regiment where it was.

It was then resolved to have recourse to new measures. Towards the end of April the above-mentioned GG. CC. met for the second time. It was proposed to concentrate a sufficient force at Naples, to be able to take the King and royal family as hostages, and conduct them to a place of safety, in order to force them to grant a liberal constitution. They swore, on the altar of the country, to preserve the highest and most inviolable respect to the sacred persons of the royal family. Their only object was to protect the throne, which had begun to totter, from ministerial perfidy. The plan was approved by all; and they turned their attention to the means of carrying it into effect.

It was then that every one sought to invite such Carbonari as were thought the most courageous, and of tried firmness, more especially those who, gifted with these qualities, could also command any force whatever, in order to further the salutary enterprize. These were, Agostino Ferrante, serjeant of the marine artillery, who invited Raffaello Villascosa, serjeant-major of the second regiment of grenadiers of the guard; Antonio Lazzaro, serjeant of the same regiment, together with Filippi Pareti; Francesco Addiechi, Serjeant-Major of the horse-artillery; Giuseppe Formica, Serjeant of the royal marine regiment; and L. Chianese, halberdier. They also invited Francesco Ranieri, of Satriano (in Calabria ultra); Ferdinando Giannone, and Raffaello Majorano, both Neapolitans. The force was then examined, and it was found to amount, between soldiers and citizens, to nearly 2000 men, all sworn sons of St. Theobald; besides the brave regiment of dragoons under the above-named Lieutenant Bologna and Captain Permasilico; and ten pieces of artillery under Addiechi, Ferrante, Scotto and Esposito.

The grenadiers of the guard were also placed in the Castel Nuovo (in which was a garrison), together with that part of King's and Queen's regiment of artillery, which, gained by the agent Pellegrini, had embraced the general cause.

It was thought fit to correspond with the provinces of the kingdom, that they might be prepared to rise on the first movements at Naples. Gagliardi, Raffaello and Marco, Scarpa and Ranieri, proceeded to Aversa, to communicate the plan, and to come to an understanding with the captain of militia Andrea Forfante, and with the captain of the Queen's regiment of cavalry Giuseppe Acerbo, both firmly attached to their country. They received the proposition with enthusiasm, &c.

The line of correspondence extended itself as far as Benevento, Sessa and S. Germano. Lieutenant Bologna, Gherardo Curci, and Tommaso Scarpa, proceeded on the same errand to Nocera, whence they passed on to Salerno, to invite the Supreme Magistracy there to act in concert. That body promised to convoke a regular meeting to answer the invitation; and two days afterwards sent the lieutenant of militia Raimondo Grimaldi, and F. B. the younger, of Rocca Piemonte (Casale of

Nocera), to Naples, through whom it conveyed an assurance, that the forces of the Carbonari in its dependence would march on the first intelligence, and that it was about to communicate the plan to the neighbouring provinces of Avellino and Basilicata. Meanwhile frequent meetings were held to mature the project; they took place for the most part in the house of Curci, where Gagliardi lived, and to which the deputations, which were constantly arriving from the provinces, repaired.

We must mention with honour, among the individuals of these deputations, the GG. CC. Domenico Cicalese, of Nocera, and Vincenzo Franco, lieutenant of the Prince's regiment of cavalry. They certified that the provinces of Avellino and of Basilicata, whither they had been sent from Salerno, as well as some corps of the army, had joined the cause. The last meeting took place on the 23d May, in the house of the G. C. Francesco Clementi de Padula, of the Principato Citra, who had resided for several years at Naples; at this meeting were present, for the first time, C. Guadalupi, and Oronce Piccioli of Lecce, and, unfortunately, Francesco Acconciagiuoco, known as a popular man; the particulars of the plot were developed to all; the oath of fidelity and firmness was renewed, and a commission of seven individuals was appointed to regulate the operations of the forces, to fix the day and hour of rising, to give the word of command, and to do all which it might deem useful to the desired end.

This commission assembled the following day, in the house of Curci and Gagliardi, and determined that the moment of the enterprize should be the night between the 29th and 30th of May.

In consequence of this decision, Curci set out to give information of it to the Magistracy of Salerno; Gagliardi proceeded to Aversa, and Gennaro de Blasiis to Marsiconuovo. The necessary orders were issued from these different points; proclamations were addressed to the army and to the people of the united kingdoms, and complete success was expected, when Acconciagiuoco revealed all to the police. On the night of the 26th May, Ferrante, Addiechi, Villascosa, Chianese, Formica, Clementi and Majorano, were surprized and imprisoned; Gagliardi, Curci and Giannone, were attacked but had time to fly; the rest fortunately escaped the vigilance of the police, because Acconciagiuoco had forgotten their names, and was ignorant where they lived. The news of this misfortune flew to the points of correspondence, and prudence determined that the proceedings should be stopped. The Princess's regiment of infantry, ready to make a retrograde movement in its march from Sicily, already begun, was obliged to proceed, in consequence of this event. It had received orders to fall back, from the Supreme Magistracy of Salerno, through the G. C. Gaetano di Pasquale of Naples, employed in the office of the Attorney General. He had the courage to abandon his situation, and to rejoin these brave men, led by the excellent G. C.

Colonel Costa, in order to unite their arms with those who were to raise the glorious standard of the Hermit Protector (St. Theobald).

Notwithstanding the most obstinate persecution, those who had escaped the danger did not relax in their ardour. Gagliardi and Curci repaired to Nocera and its environs; they agreed with the general guards (*guardie generali*), Pasquale Lombardi and P. Amabile,to fix the centre of the operations in that town, and to raise the first shout, announcing the political resurrection at that place, in the night of the 10th of June. They returned from thence to Naples, to give the necessary directions. The captain of dragoons, G. C. Rignano, the lieutenants GG. CC. Zimeo and Gennarelli, and the GG. CC. Gr. Principe P. Strina, Fr. Antonio Ceravolo (a priest), Antonio Albini and Benedetto Polvani, took part in the new enterprize; the last invited the General Vairo also to join the engagement. Gagliardi went to Aversa to re-organize that quarter. He communicated to Lombardi, at Nocera, the adherence of Vairo, and the steps taken by the G. C. Michele de Blasiis, for gaining possession of the castle of St. Elmo. Some officers of the Prince's regiment of cavalry sent the Lieutenant-Colonel to Naples, to ascertain whether Vairo persisted in his intention. Colombo confirmed it in confidence to the G. C. Tronna, of Nocera, who was then at Naples. This person, full of distrust as to the success of the affair, dissuaded Vairo by means of Polvani. A similar feeling filled the mind of the G. C. Pagliara,

President of the Supreme Magistracy of Salerno, with a panic fear; and the friends of their country saw with grief, their third project come to nothing. In the mean time Gagliardi, Curci, Principe, Guadalupo, de Blasiis, Ranieri, and Ceravolo, had repaired to Nocera. Deceived in their hopes, the three first went to the Val di Lauro, to prepare the minds of the people, and from thence to Nola, with which place they were in correspondence from the beginning; the other four returned to Naples. The Carbonari of the districts just mentioned were burning with enthusiasm; conferences took place with the excellent Abate Menechini and the brave men Morelli, Silvati, Descisciolo, and Altomare, all of the immortal Bourbon regiment of cavalry. Menechini, Silvati, Gagliardi and Curci repaired for the last time to Aversa, to confer with the captains Infante and Acerbo and several officers of the Queen's regiment of cavalry. Morelli and Principe proceeded to Naples, to consult with the officers of dragoons above-mentioned.

To ensure success, circular letters were sent from Naples to different places, to invite the Carbonari to march immediately upon the capital, according to the directions contained in those letters. They were accompanied with the seal which is now used by the general provisional assembly of the Carbonari, and which is in the custody of the G. C. Dom. Abatemarco.

Such is the account of the events which preceded the movements at Nola, of the 1st of July, which already resounds through astonished Europe, and which, consecrated in the pages of history, will be for ever admired by the remotest posterity.———

This day, the 12th of July, 1820, we, the undersigned, met together in the district (*Ordone*), of Naples, in bonds of truth and peace, swear before the Grand Master of the Universe, and upon our honour (form of Carbonarism), that the contents of this historical statement are completely true. We attest its authenticity with our signatures, accompanied with the seal of the General Provisional Assembly; and we send the original to the Supreme Magistracy of the Carbonari of the Western Lucanian Republic, in order that it may be preserved in the archives.

The Good Cousin   T. M. Gagliardi,

D. Abatemarco,

M. De Blasiis,

Gerard. Curci,

V. Bologna,

R. Scarpa,

T. Scarpa,

M. Scarpa,

Ang. Ferrante

K. Villascosa,

Fr. Addiechi,

Jos. Formica,

L. Chianese,

R. Majorano,

T. Clementi,

Nlc. Scotto,

G. Esposito,
F. Pareti,
T. Giannone.

Fr. Ranieri,	Ant. Albini,
T. Permasilico,	Ben. Polvani,
D. Cicalese,	G. Vairo, General,
Or. Piccioli,	P. Strina,
C. guadalupi,	F. Ant. Ceravolo,
G. De Pasquale,	Luigi Menechini,
S. Rignano,	M. Morelli,
I. Zimeo,	T. Silvati,
P. Gennarelli,	Gius. Descisciolo,
Gr. Principe,	Sav. Altomare.

Appendix VII

A. G. D. G. M. D. U.

The Respectable General Assembly
of the Carbonari to all the Good
Cousins of the Two

GOOD COUSINS,

ith deep grief the General Assembly thinks it necessary to announce to you, that the many outrages which are every day committed in the public roads, by low people, against peaceful travellers, as they tend to cast a stain upon the glorious epoch of our bloodless (*incruenta*) regeneration, demand that the honour and zeal of the whole population of the Carbonari should be exerted, in desiring and accomplishing their cessation.

It is true that such disorders belong unfortunately to all times, and to all nations, even to the most civilized, for where there are passions and wants, crime often takes place. It is also true that the virtuous man, and the honest citizen, should at all times feel regret and aversion for such disorders; but there are times when the same crime, from the change in circumstances, should excite greater hatred and indignation in all minds, attached to virtue, and to the glory of the age they live in.

Yes, Carbonari, this age, in which the wish of a free nation and a virtuous order alone should triumph, this age must be pure and immaculate. See how our enemies, envying our happiness, exult as they contemplate the distressing events which may diminish or destroy it. And who knows whether those enemies, always ready to obscure your glory, are not now calumniating you, and accusing you of being the quiet spectators, and, perhaps, the promoters of the disorders committed in the public highways?

Good Cousins, the General Assembly feels assured that as soon as this idea presents itself to your minds, there will not be a man among you who will not experience a feeling of horror. But this is not sufficient: inactive virtue, although it has its merits, in such cases is easily confounded with vice. Your country, your honour demand from you not regret alone, but exertion and energy, and the Assembly invites you to employ them.

Let robbers and those who commit excesses in the public ways be incessantly watched and arrested by such of you as belong to the public force, and let your calumniators know that you do not approve of crime, but eradicate it wherever it is found—be careful, however, to preserve the greatest order among yourselves, when you oppose disorder—the slightest inattention, the most trifling want of discipline, the least opposition to the public authorities may destroy the merit of the good intentions you may have, and bring upon you blame instead of honour.

Above all let there be no distinction of persons when it is your business to unite yourselves to put down excesses. Fraternal love places all the Good Cousins on the same level.

But we are speaking to Carbonari, and the path to glory is not unknown to them; this renders any further exhortation useless.

We salute you with the honours due to you.

District (Ordone) of Naples, the 24th October, 1820.
The Good Cousin President CASIGLI, Domenico.
The G. C. First Assistant ROSSAROLLI, Giuseppe.
The G. C. Second ditto CAPUANO, Buonaventura.
The G. C. Orator DORIA, Francesco.
The G. C. Secretary ROSSETTI, Gabriele.

(L. S.) The Seal represents the Goddess of Liberty, with the fasces and axe in her left hand, and with a spear bearing the cap of liberty in her right hand, treading upon a serpent—around it "*The General Assembly of the G. C. of the Two Sicilies.*"

Form of the Table of Labours[1] (extracted from the Codice della Carboneria, part 1, of the First Rank of Apprentices.

A. G. D. G. M. D. U. e del nostro Protettore S. T.

(Al Gran Dio Gran Maestro del Universo e del nostro Protettore San Teobaldo.)

To-day being the first of August in the year 300[2] of true light, being met together in a very strong and illuminated place, far from the eyes of Pagans— The Respectable Vendita, under the distinctive table of to the orders of—opens the labours in the First Rank of Apprentices. The Good Cousin N. N. holds the first axe—(There are a Grand Master and Assistants.) N. N. the second, N. N. the third. The

---

1   "*Tavola del Travagli*" is the term in Carbonarism to express the order of the day and the proceedings of the meeting.

2   This epochia corresponds with tliat ascribed to the foundation of the Society of Carbonari in the "Historical Essay on the Origin of Carbonarism," from which an extract is given in the text, namely, the reign of Francis the First of France, which reign extended from 1515 to 1547. Now the date 300 falling in with 1520, agrees well with this, and is the year of the condemnation of Luther by Leo X., and of the formation of many secret and religious societies in France and Germany, particularly that headed by Muncer, which afterwards broke out into the war of the peasantry, whose chief complaint against the nobles at that time seems to have been the severity of the Game Laws[a] a subject on which the Carbonari have more than once remonstrated and even taken up arms. —T.

a   See Jortin's *Life of Erasmus.*

Good Cousin N. N. officiates as Orator. The office of Secretary is entrusted to the Good Cousin N. N. Master of the Ceremonies, N. N. First adept (Esperto) N. N. The remaining dignitaries are noted in the margin of the present table, together with all the Good Cousins present at these labours.

Art. 1. The Grand Master examines the first assistant on the duties of his office in the Vendita, and desires him to put them in execution. This is done by means of the Master Adept (*Esperto*) and the Master of the Ceremonies.

Art. 2. The Grand Master, after regular notice, opens the labours (*travagli*) with the usual signs, salutations (*avvantaggi*) and invocations of ceremony.

Art. 3. The Grand Master, after regular notice, causes the table of past labours to be read: the same is ratified by plurality of votes.[3]

Art. 4, The Good Cousin Grand Master regularly invites the G. C. Master Adept to go into the forest, in order to see if there are any GG. CC. visitors; the same being returned, reports if there are any, and they are introduced.[4]

Art. 5, The G. M. regularly invites the G. C. Master Adept to go into the cabinet of reflection, in order to see if there are any pagans to be initiated.

---

3   If any observations are made on its articles, those observations are to be noted.

4   The number of visitors is noted in the Table, with their Christian and Surnames, country, quality, rank in the order, and the Vendita they belong to.

The same being returned, reports accordingly, and also repeats to the Vendita the answers of ceremony which they have given, such answers being conformable to justice and propriety. Art. 6. The G.M., after regular notice, causes the reception of the Pagan to be sanctioned for the last time, and invites the G. C. Master of the Ceremonies to take the necessary steps, in order that the Pagan may be introduced to the door of the Baracca.

Art. 7. A knocking is heard at the Pagan door—the G. M. asks who is the rash person that dares to disturb our sacred labours:

Art. 8. The Pagan is introduced into the Vendita, and after some questions of ceremony, the G. M. directs him to make his first journey, then the second, and afterwards the third—upon which he causes him to take the oath of ceremony.

Art. 9. The Pagan being led into the middle of the Ordoni, and the bandage being taken from his eyes, the G. M. makes him repeat his oath, and then communicates to him the signs, touch, and sacred words, and causes him to be acknowledged by the ordone.

Art. 10. The G. M. causes a salutation of ceremony to be made to the new member; the G. C. Master of the Ceremonies thanks all the GG. CC. of the Vendita for the new member, with the usual signs and salutation[s].

Art. 11. The G. C. Orator explains the symbols of the order to the new member, who thanks him with a salutation for having enlightened him.

Art. 12. The bag of propositions[5] (*sacco di proposizioni*) is sent round, which produces

Art. 13, The bag of the poor (*sacco de' poveri*) is sent round and has produced the sum (medaglia) of which is consigned to the G. C. Almoner, to use as the regulations direct. Art. 14. The G. M. regularly demands of the Ordoni if they have any observations to make on the general good of the order, and of the Vendita in particular—liberty of speech is granted.

Art. 15. The G. M. causes a salutation of ceremony to be made to the GG. CC. visitors, these thank the Vendita, and they close it (*la cuoprono.*[6]) Art. 16. The G. C. Secretary reads over the notes of the table of the present labours,—the same is ratified by the Vendita, and signed by the Dignitaries, according to custom.

Art. 17. Our forest growing dark for want of the sun, the G. M. causes the labours to be closed, with the usual signs, salutations, and invocations of ceremony.

Done and read the day, month, and year as above, and signed by us Dignitaries.[7]

FINIS

---

5 "The number, quality, and contents of the same to be explained."

6 "*Chiudono.*"

7 Here follow the signatures of the G. M., of the first and second Assistants of the Orator and Secretary.

Index

Eastern Lucanian Society 97
economists 70
Egiziani 212
Egypt 30, 223
England 2, 7, 73, 168
English Civil War 42
Esposito, G. 235
Eudes II, 5th Count of Champagne 167, 168
Europe xi, 9, 37, 63, 122, 228, 240

F

Fattiboni, Cojite Vincenzo 172, 179, 190, 194, 196
Feliziani (from Ascoli, victim of the Carbonari) 176
Fendeurs 2, 9
Fenestrella 17
Ferdinand IV of Naples; III of Sicily; and I of the Two Sicilies (from 1816) 16, 60, 61, 62, 68, 71, 77, 80, 100, 103, 106, 108, 109, 119, 123, 143, 144, 145, 157, 234, 235
Fermo 172, 174, 176, 180, 181
Ferrante, Agostino 234, 235, 237
Ferrara 57, 174, 178, 181
Field of Mars 87
Filantropi 118
Firrao, Giuseppe 213
Foggia 81
Fonsmorte (Lieutenant) 139, 141
Forfante, Andrea 235
Forli 174, 179, 187, 190
Formica, Giuseppe 234, 237
Fossanova Abbey 36

Francavilla 124, 127, 132, 133, 134, 135, 136, 139, 141, 142
Francavilla, prison of 127
France 2, 3, 7, 8, 11, 12, 13, 14, 17, 18, 62, 156, 168, 170, 246
Francesco, Doria 245
Francini, Quirino 191
Francis I, Emperor of Austria 88
Francis I of France 3, 7, 8, 246
Francis I of the Two Sicilies 109, 228
Franco, Vicenzo 236
Frederick Barbarossa 35
Free-Masonry xi, 18, 19, 70
Free-Masons 10, 69, 116, 212, 216
French Revolution 1
Fuorusciti 170

G

Gaetano di Pasquale (G. C.) 237
Gaetano (Illuminati of Ferrara) 57
Gagliardi, Francesco Maria 231, 232, 233, 235, 236, 237, 238, 239, 240
Galantina 125
Gallicia 169
Gallo d'Arpino, Cesare 13, 172, 179, 186, 190, 191, 193, 194, 195
Gargaro, Pietro 128, 129
Gatti (Carbonaro) 42
General Assembly of the Carbonari 108
Gennarelli, P. 238, 241
Genoa 11, 12, 14, 17

254

L

M